mentoring
wisdom
living and leading well

DR. CARSON PUE

Foreword by Doug Birdsall

CASTLE QUAY BOOKS

Mentoring Wisdom- Living and Leading Well

Published by:
Castle Quay Books
1307 Wharf Street, Pickering, Ontario, L1W 1A5
Tel: (416) 573-3249
E-mail: info@castlequaybooks.com
www.castlequaybooks.com

Copy edited by: Marina H. Hofman Willard
Cover design by: Essence Design
Printed at Essence Printing, Belleville, Ontario

Library and Archives Canada Cataloguing in Publication

Pue, Carson, 1955-
    Mentoring wisdom : living and leading well / Carson Pue.

Includes bibliographical references and index.
Issued also in electronic format.

ISBN 978-1-894860-51-2
1. Leadership—Religious aspects—Christianity. 2. Christian life. I. Title.

BV4597.53.L43P83 2011   248.8'8   C2011-903951-6

TABLE OF CONTENTS

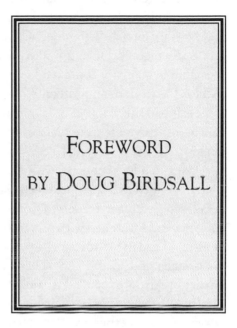

FOREWORD
BY DOUG BIRDSALL

MANY BOOKS HAVE BEEN WRITTEN ABOUT MENTORING, BUT FEW COMBINE THE wisdom born of life experience with the wisdom of Scripture, all beautifully woven together in the context of prayer. But this is precisely what Carson Pue has done. Carson Pue is a globally respected mentor who has made a life-long study of mentors and mentoring. As you read this book, his command of this field will become increasingly evident to you. However, this book is not so much a book *about* mentoring as it is a truly original exemplar *of* mentoring.

Mentoring Wisdom will be valuable for a long time to leaders around the world because of the comprehensive scope of the more than one hundred issues and situations that Carson addresses and for the way in which each issue is addressed with such clarity and brevity. As a bonus to the reader, the leadership themes are neatly indexed so that you can readily obtain wisdom on an issue that is immediately before you.

In a very real sense, I have been "reading" this book over the course of nearly two decades. During that time, I have seen the ideas come into clearer focus. I have listened as the insights have grown deeper and as the wisdom has matured to greater richness. Carson Pue is a friend and a colleague with whom I have shared the journey of life and ministry for 20 years.

We meet together annually for a week with a group of about 15 colleagues from around the world. We have met together in Europe, Australia, Asia and North America. This group was formed by Leighton Ford, himself a wise and godly mentor. Having walked with Carson all these years, and having seen him in so many contexts, I can speak for the authenticity of the book and for the wisdom and integrity of its author.

As I read this book, as it is now to be published, I have the sense of sitting across the table from Carson and listening to him reflect on the challenges that face a servant leader. I have seen him navigate the challenges of serving in a local church, with the agony and ecstasy which that entails. I have watched as he assumed leadership for a young ministry committed to developing younger leaders. I listened to him share his dreams and his struggles and I watched with admiration as he grew and developed the work of Arrow Leadership into a visionary enterprise of national prominence in his Canada and in the U.S. Then, I watched as the vision grew and the impact of Arrow expanded to a place of global influence.

In October of 2010, Carson and I and our colleagues in the Point Group were together in Cape Town for the Third Lausanne Congress where over 4,000 leaders from 198 countries had gathered together for ten days to consider the issues of paramount importance to the church with respect to world evangelization. Three things struck me about my time together with Carson at Cape Town 2010. First, I was struck by the repeated references by speakers at the Congress to the priority of godly leadership and the need for wise mentors. Second, I could not help but notice the many younger leaders from around the world who were there who had been impacted by Carson's vision and the ethos of Arrow Leadership. Thirdly, and most encouragingly, I had a growing sense of hope for the future of the Church as I saw the qualities of Christ-like leadership which were being nurtured in the lives of people impacted by Carson and his wife, Brenda, and those who are part of the Arrow Leadership global network. They are people with a passion for evangelism and a foundational commitment to be led more by Jesus, leading more like Jesus, all for the purpose of leading more to Jesus.

As I have served as a missionary in Asia since 1980 and as I have traveled the world the last several years on behalf of the Lausanne Movement, I am increasingly convinced that the greatest needs are not primarily about new strategies and programs, nor are they about better buildings, more personnel, additional financial resources, and innovative use of technology, as important as these issues are. No, the greatest need is for leaders, men and women with Christ-like character, faith and vision. These leaders, whether born or made, must be developed over time. Furthermore, the most helpful means by which this is accomplished is through the gift of a wise and godly mentor. *Mentoring Wisdom* is such a gift. It will be a source of wisdom for younger leaders, while at the same time being a sourcebook for more seasoned leaders. I welcome and commend this mature contribution from my friend and colleague, Carson Pue. Read it slowly, perhaps just one section a day. Reflect, pray and let the wisdom take root in your own heart and practice. When you have complete reading this book, read it again. Then pass it on. God bless you!

S. Douglas Birdsall
Executive Chair, The Lausanne Movement
Boston, Massachusetts
July 2011

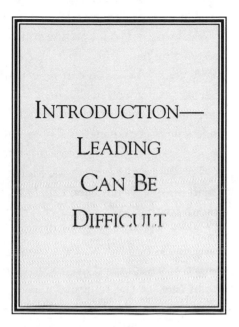

INTRODUCTION— LEADING CAN BE DIFFICULT

THE ROLE OF BEING A LEADER IS A VERY DIFFICULT ONE. OFTEN, WE ARE CALLED upon to give wisdom and direction, inspiration and hope, vision and paths of execution. Where does all this come from? It comes from a pool of collective wisdom that is gathered over time.

For Christian leaders, it comes from our ability to call upon God to provide us with the wisdom and discernment we need at a particular time. Every great leader that I have met also has a series of mentors in their life who are providing or have provided wisdom. This wisdom becomes part of the pool from which we draw as leaders.

Many leaders today wish that they had a mentor in their life. Someone who loves them, cares about their leadership and mission, listens carefully to their leadership challenges, and provides reflective feedback that points them both to God and the way forward. Yet, all too often, men and women find themselves without this great resource. This book is intended to serve as a passive mentor. A passive mentor is one that we can glean knowledge from, even though we may never meet him or her personally.

The following pages contain a collection of insights that speak into challenges faced by most leaders. Included with each is a scriptural verse or passage that points us toward faith and God's promise to walk with us through each day that we lead.

As I write to you, I picture you, as a leader, sitting at your desk with this book sitting near the corner of a writing pad. Or maybe you have found a comfy chair where you can reflect awhile. It is the beginning of the week and, as a leader, you need a little inspiration to get the week going. Imagine a mentor sitting across from you and caring about your week to come. The leadership issues covered will often intersect with what you are facing. These are real issues and they come out of my own life.

For the past several years, I have been publishing a monthly leadership e-mail missive. It has been based on exactly what I am going through at the time of writing. As a leader of a ministry organization with outlets around the globe, I know of the challenging days that leaders face. As a mentor to many ministry leaders, I also know of the power that can be found in collective wisdom and hearing from the Word of God.

In each of the topics addressed, I will be asking you a question about yourself or your leadership while also providing some leadership insights I have learned while leading Arrow Leadership. We will close each section with a prayer that you might use as a guide in your own prayers for the week that follows. I suggest that you add a three minute moment of silence after reading each prayer. Invite God to speak to you and enjoy the peace of His presence.

My prayer is that these insights will provide you with a needed updraft under the wings of leadership in whatever you face this day. These topics are also well suited for discussion with your team. So, watch for opportunities to apply these mentoring nuggets in your own life and organizational context. I would love to hear your stories of how God uses these words to help further the work of your church, organization or business for the sake of His kingdom.

Here to help you grow,
Carson Pue
carsonp@arrowleadership.org

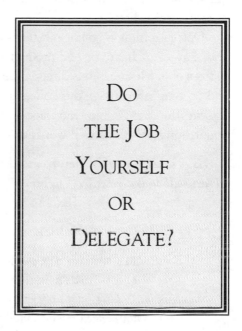

Do the Job Yourself or Delegate?

IT'S A DILEMMA WE ALL FACE. DO YOU COMPLETE A SMALL TASK YOURSELF OR teach someone else? You know it's easier to do the job yourself, but your schedule is too full. Giving it to a subordinate will require explanation, training and time. Which way to go?

There are pros and cons for training someone else. Sometimes parameters around deadlines and quality of work can prohibit you from delegating to a colleague. But please pause to consider the valuable leadership development opportunities available when delegating.

The most obvious and direct benefit of delegating is that the subordinate learns the skill. It's the old maxim, "Give a man a fish and he eats for a day; teach a man to fish and he eats for a lifetime." Often, we decide against the time and effort to teach someone a skill if we think it will only be used once. I suggest that this is a shortsighted and selfish view.

With our heavy workload, we want to seek the easiest path to completing a task. But doing a quick task yourself may deny the opportunity to build up your team. Working with subordinates to develop their skill level is an inherent responsibility of leadership. Certainly completing tasks

11

quickly and independently is good, but investing time and effort with our subordinates is better!

Delegation takes courage. It takes more effort, will probably take longer, and may even have an end-product quality cost. But remember that the success of our leadership is directly related to the competence, commitment and accomplishments of our colleagues.

So the next time you face this dilemma, see it as a leadership opportunity. It will be well worth the effort.

> *"But select capable men from all the people—men who fear God...*
> *That will make your load lighter, because they will share it with you."*
> (Exodus 18:21-22, NIV)

O Lord,

I admit that something happens to me when I think about involving others in projects and tasks. It makes sense in my head to involve others, so I don't fully understand why I delay in doing so. I know that You have called me personally to lead and you have also called others to be a part of this great work. I can even think of examples where I know that You have revealed part of the picture to one person and another part to another person, so it makes perfect sense to involve others in discerning counsel, guidance and direction.

I recognize that I struggle with perfectionism. While circumstances sometimes require me to act without consulting others, there is a danger of arrogance and error that can come from proceeding on my own. Please give me eyes to see the help that You have placed around me. Forgive me for forgetting that You are the only one who is perfect. Give me that courage to delegate, the grace to allow learning, and the love and care of my colleagues that is so encompassing I would dare not fail to share the load with them.

Amen

GENEROUS ENCOURAGEMENT

HOW IMPORTANT IT IS FOR YOU TO FEEL ENCOURAGED?

How important is it for you, as a leader, to then offer encouragement?

People today need more encouragement than ever. Why? Life can be discouraging. We live in a society that can chew leaders up and spit them out. The "high-tech" age has forgotten how to be "high-touch." All of this can be terribly discouraging.

But encouragement blesses both the recipient and the giver. It is so motivating that the slightest touch—a note, a call, a smile—can spark great accomplishments.

Leaders encourage! Acts 20 tells us of Paul travelling through Macedonia "speaking many words of encouragement to the people." Yet, on the continuum between encouragement and criticism many of us need to confess to spending more time criticizing others rather than encouraging them.

Do you know of one in need of some financial encouragement? Perhaps a single parent struggling to gain back self-assurance, a student away at school, a newly married couple just establishing their home, a forgotten servant of the Lord working hard in a difficult ministry? Do you know of one who needs a word of encouragement?

Be generous with your encouragement! Add the spark!

*"And do not forget to do good and to share with others,
for with such sacrifices God is pleased."*
(Hebrews 13:16, NIV)

O Lord,

Grant me this day freedom from self-centeredness. May I be energized and motivated by my personal relationship with You, O God, so that I will see people as You see them and engage in acts that will encourage those around me. May my experience of Your love compel me to share that love through encouraging actions and words. As my mind reflects on my numerous contacts, bring to mind, Lord, those that need that spark of encouragement today. Make me particularly sensitive to those closest to me, that I might not overlook them. Use me today as Your vessel to offer living water. Thank You for the many people in my life who have offered encouragement along the way. May I do likewise. Help me to keep the busyness of work at bay in order to allow a nudge from You when there is someone that You want encouraged. I offer myself to You this day to be used in someone's life. Make me a beacon of hope and save me from my tendency to be critical, especially when I am tired. May I, as Your servant, offer encouragement to those I meet no matter how commonplace or insignificant it may seem at the time. May You use these moments for Your greater purpose in their lives.

Amen

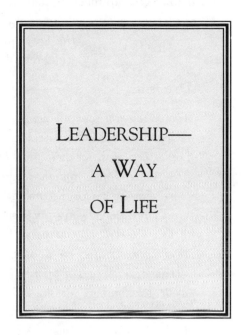

LEADERSHIP—
A WAY
OF LIFE

LEADERSHIP IS NOT A ROLE, BUT A WAY OF LIVING THAT PERMEATES everything we do and are.

We commonly assume that leadership is a quality or ability of a person rather than a relational experience that transforms people. This assumption may keep us from engaging in some of the more difficult aspects, such as shared leadership, self-managing teams, and decision making at the operational level.

The emerging leaders we are working with seem to be hard-wired for relational ministry. They create leadership through their interactions and focus on "shared meaning" for others. It is a process by which people participate in leadership together and one that acknowledges that leaders do not exist without followers.

Leadership is all about relationships.

Jesus practiced a relational style of leadership. He led his disciples by sharing life with them. In fact, in the second and third year of His ministry He actually gave them more time, not less. How about you?

What time do you have available this week to invest in relationships?

For those you have worked closely with over time—are you giving them more or less of your time?

"Let us not give up meeting together, as some are in the habit of doing, but let us encourage one another—and all the more as you see the Day approaching."
(Hebrews 10:25, NIV)

Dear Jesus,

Thank You for Your relationship with me. I know that You are a relational God. My life would be empty were You not my Savior and Lord. Forgive me for those times in the past when I have withdrawn from people—often from the relationships that should mean the most to me. Forgive me for succumbing to temptations that rob me of time I could intentionally invest in people. Increase within me the capacity to love deeply and faithfully. Bring into the light of Your love anything that causes me to be afraid of intimacy or keeps me from making relationships a priority in my life. Help me also to learn about relationships afresh. Are there things I should be doing differently? What can I learn from the emerging generation? What do You have to say to me, Lord?

I know that leaders are often measured by their accomplishments. Forgive me for the many times I care more about the project than the people. Prod me when I need to be reminded that at the end of my time on earth my measure will be found more in the relationships left behind than any project, building or wealth. Help me as I am juggling the many occupational demands of a leader and remind me that You worked in community as You walked the same earth upon which I walk. I know that the people around me want to be loved. Help me to take the initiative to love and serve them in gentleness and humility.

Amen

BLOCKED VISION

DO YOU SENSE A GREAT DISTANCE BETWEEN WHERE YOU ARE NOW AND WHERE you want to be?

If "yes," then be encouraged! It means you have a vision. God uses the vision of where you want to be to draw you forward and to help you overcome obstacles.

In my experience, vision seldom comes as a brilliant flash. Usually, it emerges from our everyday prayers and thinking—where God combines our logic and intuition, thoughts and feelings, past and present experience—to give us a glimpse of future potential.

Be aware of the things that block vision:

> **Too much activity or pressure.** Vision needs space and often quiet.
> **Poor self-concept.** You are God's child. Don't devalue your ideas or yourself.
> **Fear of failure.** It can seem safer to not pursue a vision.
> **Forgetting.** Find a way of capturing your ideas and visions.
> **Journal!**

Lack of focus. Visionaries often have more than one vision. Work on one at a time.

Imbalance. Vision combines head and heart. It is logical and spiritual.

Tiredness. Unless it is a dream in our sleep, we have trouble being visionary when we are tired.

Vacation times can be wonderfully filled with vision, as we stop the busyness of our lives long enough to address many of these vision blockers.

> *"After this, the word of the LORD came to Abram in a vision: 'Do not be afraid, Abram. I am your shield, your very great reward.'"*
> (Genesis 15:1, NIV)

Dear Jesus,

Early in Your ministry, You called Your disciples to leave everything and follow You. Your sense of vision was so strong and well communicated that people actually left their families and businesses in order to follow You. I want to communicate vision from You that has that kind of impact on the people I lead. Yet today, Lord, I feel blocked from that vision. Reveal to me those things that prevent me from hearing clearly from You and communicating it to others.

I long to share with people a vision for something bigger than themselves and to be able to communicate that in ways they can grasp. I want to be the type of leader that will help equip those who follow me to fulfill Your vision. Forgive me for how often I give modest attention to many things and enable me to search out Your vision in such a way that all else fades away and disappears. May I allow a ringing phone to go unanswered or an e-mail without a response when I am seeking that deeper call from You.

In the past, when I have been on a quest for Your vision, my search has been generously rewarded. Help me today to pay attention to those things that have Your attention. Provide me with the clues that I need to begin to see the true picture and deep secrets of what You want done. Free me of any preconditions about how this will happen and allow me to experience You by being open to the mystical and divine, with the expectation that You will appear and provide vision.

Amen

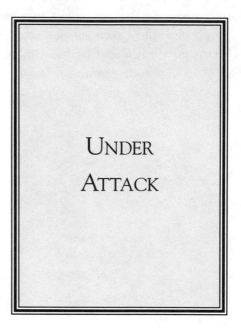

UNDER ATTACK

DO YOU HAVE SOMETHING BEARING DOWN ON YOU TODAY? IS IT SIGNIFICANT, even critical?

Leaders are under attack on three fronts:

> **At the office**—expectations and competition are forcing organizations to search for ways of increasing productivity.
>
> **At home**—the lack or breakdown of relationships exerts further pressures rather than bringing relief and support.
>
> **Spiritually**—time pressures squeeze out the cultivation of a satisfying spiritual life and rob leaders of intimacy with God.

Every leader I know has a tremendous workload. But it is not the load that breaks you down—it's the way you carry it. John Wesley said, "Though I am always in haste, I am never in a hurry, because I never undertake any more work than I can get through with perfect calmness of spirit." And Wesley led the greatest revival ever, in Britain!

If you are in a situation or environment that is fraught with emotional or social pressures that are distracting you, then seek calmness of spirit. The Bible says it this way, "Number our days."

This is an important growth area for us as leaders. Often, we become so focused on what is immediately in front of us that we lose perspective. Very often wisdom comes to us when we simply stop and ask for God's perspective.

When you start feeling overwhelmed, try to "number your days." Look at today through the lens of your vision or calling. We need to keep our eyes fixed on a further horizon in order to find the right pathway there. What will you do today to number your days?

> *"Teach us to number our days aright,*
> *that we may gain a heart of wisdom."*
> (Psalm 90:12, NIV)

Heavenly Father,

I acknowledge my feelings of being overwhelmed. It seems like such a heavy burden to bear. Things are pressing in on me and almost crushing the life out of me as a leader at every opportunity. I feel like I have been under a heavy load for too long and have become frustrated, impatient, and sometimes unkind to people around me. Forgive me, Lord, for trying to control the things that Your Spirit wants to accomplish through me.

I also acknowledge, Lord, that many of the things I am up against are invisible. I am leading in the context of a titanic spiritual war where the opposing forces of darkness attack any effort I might make for the sake of Your kingdom. Protect me and those around me.

Leadership is so complex—help me to know what to say yes to and what requires a firm no. I relinquish my current circumstances to You and ask that You make sense of all the demands I am feeling this day.

Amen

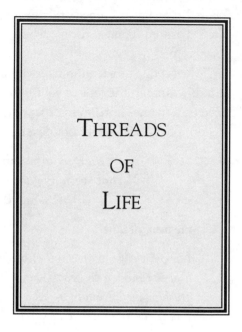

THREADS OF LIFE

As this day on the calendar flips by, we weave one more thread into the cable of our lives. If this cable is made up of our habits, thoughts and behaviors, what have you been weaving into your life this past year? Are there some threads that you need to cut?

It is good to take time to reflect on barriers to our leadership and then to commit to doing something about them. Not surprisingly, this is where most of us get stuck. Leaders often feel a sense of fatigue and can easily be overwhelmed. The future can look blurry as we consider needed growth and change during times of introspection.

If you are feeling a little blocked in this way, let me suggest a new approach. Try thinking about the needs around you and ask yourself, "What needs would benefit from my attention? What do I see around me that I am particularly competent to meet and that I am deeply concerned about?" Ask God to place some specific needs on your heart and then give focus, prayer and effort to responding to them.

Now, begin to create a plan to meet those needs. Part of the difference between leaders and others is simply having a plan. Committing ourselves to a plan moves us beyond promises and hope. So get planning!

"Commit to the LORD whatever you do, and your plans will succeed."
(Proverbs 16:3, NIV)

O Lord,

Receive all of my leadership, my intellect, my intuitions, my understanding, and my entire will. Everything that I have, all the things that I call my own, You have given to me. This day I return it all to You. Everything I have is Yours. Do with it and with me what You will.

I know I have to plan, but I desire plans that come from You. Create within me a passion for those things You are deeply concerned about. Use the skills and talents You have woven within me to create an effective plan. Protect me from that temptation that distructs me, beguiles me or forces me off the path that You have directed. Strengthen my character so that I might surmount all barriers and be enlightened to the seductions of ideas that have nothing to do with Your will. Make me especially aware of those ideas that are good and useful, but not meant for this time.

Thank You for the privilege of leadership. It is a responsibility I take seriously, as one under Your authority. Once the plan is in place, may I be disciplined enough to obey. With Your help and guidance, Lord, I shall not depart from it.

Amen

BEAUTY OF SOLITUDE

I CANNOT BE THE LEADER I SHOULD BE WITHOUT TIMES OF SOLITUDE.

This has taken me years to realize. By nature I am a people person, so the concept of solitude does not come naturally. At first it was almost painful, but now I long for time alone.

Have you ever noticed how some of our best ideas come to us while we are in the shower? Why? Because it is one of the few places left in our lives where we are alone.

We live in an action-packed, noisy environment, yet are expected to lead with clear thinking. I believe our clearest thinking occurs in silence. Solitude provides us the opportunity to be quiet. My journal is filled with examples of clear thinking, written while I visited a quiet spot—a tree-lined mountain lake, a chair in our family room or on the front porch early in the morning.

Vision is birthed in solitude. Yes, there are moments when God inspires vision while we are with others, but vision is usually delineated in the sanctuary of solitude.

Doesn't it make sense to invest a small amount of time in solitude to make the rest of your leadership more effective?

Ask yourself: How often am I completely alone? Is it enough time to meet my leadership needs? Do I allow myself to be silent? Do I have a quiet spot? Am I willing?

"For thus the Lord GOD, the Holy One of Israel, has said, 'In repentance and rest you will be saved. In quietness and trust is your strength.' But you were not willing."
(Isaiah 30:15, NASB)

Lord,

As a leader, I find myself constantly surrounded by people. It seems I am seldom alone. Life is busy, noisy and often cluttered with tasks and unfinished projects. Am I afraid of being quiet? Is my day booked so full with appointments that I have neglected to make an appointment to be alone with You? Forgive me for the way I've used my time.

If I am going to surrender myself and this organization freely to Your leadership, I know I need more times of solitude. I remember and love the times that we have shared in the mystical oneness that accompanies times of silence in Your presence. I long for more of these moments to increase my faith, hope and love. May our times together increase my sense of Your presence in all of life's events.

Lord, I want to make an appointment with You today for—a time of calmness, recollection and detachment from the pressures of today—a time where all I sense is Your love and where I am filled with Your sense of order, Your peace and Your understanding of time. Help me this day to quiet all of the thoughts that fill my head— the appointments, the meetings, and the "to-do" list. Help me to clearly understand that You are in control and nothing is more important than what You want to say to me in a time of silence.

Amen

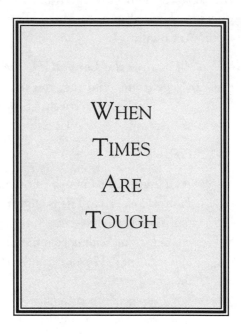

WHEN TIMES ARE TOUGH

EVERY LEADER WILL FACE TIMES WHEN IT SEEMS THAT EVERYTHING IS FALLING apart.

Whether set off by external events or internal mistakes, a crisis can be a distressing time. The emotions of everyone on the team are thrown into turmoil as past hard work and the future are at once placed in jeopardy. Everyday work gets more difficult as people lose focus and worry about the dire consequences the crisis could bring.

It is precisely at times like these that leaders emerge. A business leader from Montreal reminded me today, "When times are great, there are lots of leaders—every vision works! But when times are tough—that's when you see true leadership."

The leader has to be the one who remains cool under pressure. The one who behind closed doors is on bended knees asking God for wisdom, guidance and support. The leader has to be the one who consolidates people and resources, identifies alternatives, selects the best course of action and confidently works toward fulfilling the mission. The leader is the one who also tries to help each teammate deal with the emotions of the moment. The leader needs to show his or her people the light at the end of the tunnel with a confident plan that moves successfully beyond current circumstances.

To be an exceptional leader, you need to prepare well before the tough times hit. You should have a solid awareness of what to do and how to act during a crisis so that you can move forward in confidence when the pressure is on. Here are some leadership tips for tough times:

Focus on your vision. Economic malaise is temporary, as is economic vigor. It's your vision that's permanent, with its associated mission, values and strategy. Ensure it is sound, and reiterate it to your team.

Sharpen your core competencies. Every ministry or organization has a unique and special calling that differentiates it from others. Sharpen yours.

Bring good people alongside. During any economic downturn you truly find out who your friends are. Get together with them, seeking counsel, wisdom and partnerships.

Redeploy. When times are tough, redeploy the best people to lead initiatives suited to their gifts. Are there volunteers who can assist? Is there a new way for you to deliver your services?

Guard your cash. Use money prudently to maintain current operations and invest it wisely for the future, including the future hiring of new employees.

Manage your knowledge. Capture, process, disseminate and leverage your unique knowledge. Strengthen your knowledge and relationship management systems or, if you don't have any, develop them.

Eliminate the valueless. Now is the time to cull the activities that don't enhance core values, to reengineer your processes, and to ruthlessly eliminate anything wasteful.

While it never feels good, negative downturns are learning experiences that will strengthen you for the future. The intense heat and pressure of a crisis both refines and purifies you as a leader.

> *"Before I was afflicted I went astray: but now I have kept thy word."*
> (Psalm 119:67, KJV)

Lord,

I have been at this long enough to acknowledge both the joys and the heartaches of leadership. Help me as a leader to manage well the emotions of both the extremes. During difficult seasons help me not to take my work too seriously or to become discouraged by the hard work required at this time.

I believe that You can take all situations and use them for good. Thank You for selecting me as a leader to guide during this time. It's tough, Lord, and I cannot do it alone. Perhaps that's one of the good things that comes out of difficult times—it forces me to my knees and creates a willingness to hear from You.

Lord, I want to hold onto my work loosely. I recognize that You are my true source of significance and security—not my job or my role. But tough times often call for hard work, so help me to put the pieces together, to be realistic about my workload, generous with people and filled with creativity that brings productivity, positive changes, pride of accomplishment and enjoyable and fun relationships amidst the challenges. I know that You are preparing us for the future. May You find me ready and willing.

Amen

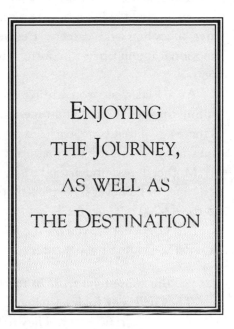

Enjoying the Journey, as Well as the Destination

ONE OF THE MORE DIFFICULT CHALLENGES THAT LEADERS FACE IS LEARNING to appreciate the journey, not just the destination. If a leader is visionary and can see a desired future, he or she can find it hard to live in the present and create a path that will get him or her there.

Columbia University researcher Walter Mischel gave a test to four-year-olds. In the test, he took each child alone into a room where a marshmallow was waiting on a plate. He told each child, "You can have this marshmallow now, but if you wait until I come back, you can have two marshmallows." Then he left.

Hidden cameras recorded each child's reactions. Some kids gobbled the marshmallow immediately, unable to resist the temptation. Some lasted a few minutes before diving in. However, there were some children who were determined to wait until Mischel returned. They would sing songs, play games, cover their eyes, and some even slept, to prevent themselves from eating the marshmallow before he returned. He returned about 20 minutes later—an eternity to a four-year-old.

He calculated and recorded the test results. Then he followed their lives for 20 years to see if there was a significant correlation between each child's test results and their measure of success in life. The findings revealed that those who could hold out for the reward were much more successful in their later schooling and careers. Delayed gratification requires considerable emotional intelligence to control impulses and devise clever ways to self-soothe.

As a leader, are you willing to wait for two marshmallows? Are you willing to take one step at a time to achieve the vision God has given you? Is there a goal that you have been pressing toward, perhaps too hard, because you want to get to the destination?

Mother Teresa understood that great accomplishments happen one step at a time. "If I'd never have picked up the first person, I'd never have picked up the 42,000 in Calcutta."

Let me encourage you on the journey. Wait and take it a step at a time, in order to achieve even greater results.

> **"But those who trust in the LORD will find new strength.**
> **They will soar high on wings like eagles. They will run and not**
> **grow weary. They will walk and not faint."**
> (Isaiah 40:31, NLT)

Gracious God,

It is so hard for me to wait. I can see a vision for the future, and it is so difficult for me to wait for You to act. I want my prayers answered now and watch daily for the open doors that will lead us forward. During the time of waiting, it seems that all I can think of is having what it is I am waiting for.

I admit that, at times, I feel downright weary of asking and waiting. At my lowest moments I wonder if You are refusing me or sometimes I get insecure about Your reasons for not answering my prayers. Deep inside I know that You want my best and that Your time is not my time. I know all of this—but still have trouble waiting.

Help me to enjoy where I am at right now and savour this part of the journey. Give me insights as to how I can continue to step forward. Deepen my faith in You, O Lord, during the times when my heart longs for what can only come in the fullness of time. Give me a calm assurance that Your will for me is grander than anything I could ever imagine. Still my mind and heart in Your love so that I am mindful of the grace You are draping around me every single day, every single moment. I ask this for Your sake.

Amen

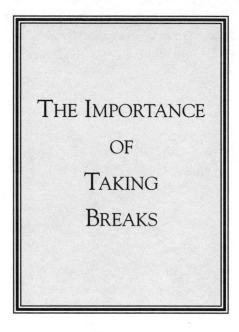

THE IMPORTANCE OF TAKING BREAKS

EXPEDIA.COM TAKES AN ANNUAL VACATION DEPRIVATION SURVEY TO TRY TO determine the patterns of their customers. What do they find? North Americans don't take vacations often enough and are leaving an average of four vacation days unclaimed per year. Add to this finding that when we do go away on holiday we often bring work along with us, thus keeping our minds essentially engaged in that which we are trying to take a break from.

Leaders must act differently and model the value of taking breaks. Here is why:

Breaks promote creativity. A good vacation can help us to reconnect with ourselves and help us get back to feeling our best. During breaks our minds are freed up to think differently—so keep your journal nearby and capture the ideas.

Breaks stave off burnout. Leaders who take regular time to relax are less likely to experience burnout, making them more creative and productive than their overworked, under-rested counterparts.

Breaks can keep us healthy. Taking regular time off to

"recharge your batteries" reduces stress levels and keeps you healthier.

Breaks can strengthen bonds. Spending time enjoying life with loved ones can keep relationships strong. It allows you to enjoy the good times more and strengthens you for the stress of hard times.

God modelled breaks both in the creation story, when we are told that on the seventh day He rested, and through the example of Jesus who, in the New Testament, consistently spends time alone in quiet places. The Bible actually commands us to make a life pattern of taking "Sabbath" breaks.

The bottom line is that taking a good amount of time away from the stresses of daily leadership can give us the break we need so that we can return to our role refreshed and better equipped to handle whatever comes.

Most leaders I interact with have an enlarged capacity for working hard. Taking a break allows us to remember who we are and to Whom we belong. In our culture, where time has become a commodity, remembering who we are is sometimes a challenge. Sabbath keeping may be more important than ever. It is vital for all people, especially leaders.

So let me invite you to slow down and to reclaim Sabbath time. (If you are looking for something to read while you are away, pick up *The Rest of God: Restoring Your Soul by Restoring Sabbath* by Mark Buchanan.)

"Six days let work be done, but on the seventh day take your rest:
at plowing time and at the grain-cutting you are to have a day for rest."
(Exodus 34:21, BBE)

O Lord of the Sabbath,

Teach me how to take a break and truly rest from my work. Help me to cease striving. Too often these days I find myself accomplishing little, not because I have nothing to do, but because there are too many things to do and I am overwhelmed.

On my time off this week, let me rest at Your feet and worship You in my stillness. I long to be still enough to hear Your Holy Spirit whisper to me and restore my soul, which has become weary from the past week of work. Refresh my spirit with the beauty of Your word. Help me to find refuge in You, that I may be a refuge for others in their struggles.

I surrender to You all of my worries and work. I sacrifice to You my need for control and ask You to take this day to lead me beside still waters. I praise you and I love you, God of rest. In You alone I am justified and not by the works of my own hand.

Amen

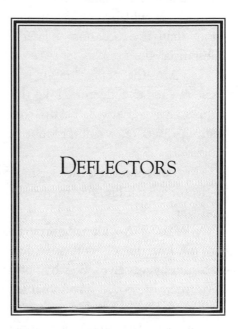

DEFLECTORS

WHILE ON OUR SAILBOAT, A LEADER RECENTLY ASKED ME, "WHAT IS THAT?" He was pointing up one of the mast stays (cable holding the mast upright).

"That's a radar deflector," I replied.

"Why do you need that?" the land-lover puzzled.

"Well," I smiled, "Sailboats don't show up very well on radar because they are low to the water. With that radar deflector hoisted up there it makes us look like an aircraft carrier."

I thought about this conversation afterwards in this light. The radar deflector makes us appear to be something we aren't, and there are many leaders who in essence carry around deflectors like this in their life and leadership. We find ways to deflect people from finding out who we really are.

You have probably run into leaders like these. You're trying to get to know them, but all they do is tell you about what they do. Others deflect through their choice of clothing or jewelry. We can also deflect by sharing our vision or talking about our organization or ministry in a way that is like a press release rather than a proper reflection of reality.

I am often suspicious when I hear leaders consistently referring to numbers as evidence of effectiveness. Yes, that may be one metric, but on more than one occasion, I later discovered that their numbers are not substantiated.

So why the deflection? It is usually an insecurity that causes us to raise our radar deflectors. Like the sailboat, it can be a means of having others give you a wide berth—keeping people at arm's length. If we are feeling insecure, we don't want people to know that reality for fear of rejection.

Insecurity breeds misleadership. So let me ask you, "Do you have a radar deflector in your life? Are there ways that you keep people from knowing the real you?"

Most of us do. It is a maturing process to be able to recognize it and work towards lowering our deflective defenses. Awareness is key and usually hard to attain by ourselves. So why not try this? Ask someone very close to you, "Are there ways you have observed me keeping people from knowing the real me?" Or, for your organization or ministry, "Are there ways we are communicating with people or supporters that keep them from knowing the reality of our ministry outcomes?"

Tough questions, yet helpful in generating real growth in leaders. My observation is that leaders are usually not able to face these questions until their late 40s or 50s. It would be wonderful if we could get to that point earlier.

> **"When Jesus saw Nathanael approaching, he said of him,**
> **'Here is a true Israelite, in whom there is nothing false.'"**
> (John 1:47, NIV)

Heavenly Father,

With Your abundant kindness, grant me this request—that my thoughts, my words and my deeds, all of my motives and my feelings, conscious and unconscious, manifest and hidden, be unified in truth and sincerity, without a trace of self-deception.

Purify my heart and sanctify me. Sprinkle me with the waters of purification and wash me clean with Your kindness and love. Make me so aware of Your steadfast love that I will be in awe at all times and in all places. I want to rely on You always as I go about my daily life.

Protect me from all hypocrisy, pride, anger, vindictiveness, lying and self-deception. Protect me from everything that is damaging to holiness and the purity of my leadership and service for You. I want to be real with You and all those I love and serve.

Amen

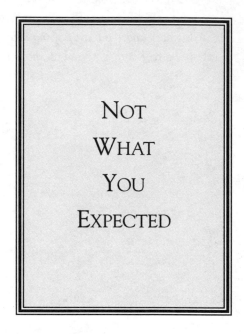

NOT WHAT YOU EXPECTED

HOW IS YOUR LIFE GOING? I MEAN, HOW IS IT REALLY GOING?

Brenda and I undertook a kitchen renovation. Everyone I know who has ever done a renovation tried to wave me off this project. Here are some comments I received:

> "Take whatever timeline they gave you and multiply it by six and then take whatever budget you have and double it."

> "Whenever I hear of a couple doing a home renovation I begin praying for their marriage. So I want you to know I am praying for you and Brenda."

> "The renovation will lead you to things that you never expected."

> And one of my favorites, "I give you three months." For what? I replied. "Until you will be getting new appliances!"

Being the leader that I am and despite these warnings, I was going to have us in and out of this in one week. Well, three weeks into it and we were only halfway through—so the six times any deadline was proving to be true.

What happens in a renovation is what happens to us all the time as leaders. You go to make a change in one area and you uncover something else that needs changing. We wanted to replace our vinyl floor covering and discovered that it was installed in a manner that meant we would have to lay a new subfloor. This then led to us having to install new subfloor throughout (not just the kitchen), which then meant replacing the floor moldings, etc. I could go on, as every aspect of this renovation has been like that. Those of you familiar with such projects know the drill.

Few things are more crushing or depressing for us as leaders than when we find that our lives and leadership are uncovering things we had not expected. It is a very vulnerable moment—those times when you find yourself thinking deeply, "Well, I didn't expect this to happen."

> Your health starts to fail.
> A valued colleague decides to leave your team.
> Your child makes wrong choices, in spite of faithful, loving parenting.
> Funding you were counting on was redirected.

The apostle Paul can resonate with how you feel. He was profoundly conscious of challenges as a minister for Christ. "Since through God's mercy we have this ministry, we do not lose heart" (2 Corinthians 4:1, NIV). He knew the crushing burden of things not going as he expected. Beaten, stoned, shipwrecked, in constant physical danger, on frequent journeys, toil, hardships, sleepless nights, hunger, thirst and exposure to cold (2 Corinthians 11:24-28). That's his list.

Do you not think that, at times, he wanted to throw his hands in the air and say, "I didn't sign up for this!"? You bet he did! So be encouraged by his leadership and triumphantly assertion: "We do not lose heart. Though outwardly we are wasting away, yet inwardly we are being renewed day by day.

**"We are hard pressed on every side,
but not crushed."**
(2 Corinthians 4:8, NIV)

Heavenly Father,

Your Word reminds me that I can be afflicted in every way, but not crushed; perplexed but not forsaken; struck down but not destroyed; always carrying in me the death of Jesus, so that the life of Jesus may be made visible in my life. Help me to be the living expression of this as I journey along in my leadership.

Today, Lord, I will remember to look to You first and foremost before I start anything. I want to trust Your plans for me. I anticipate new beginnings that might emerge from what You uncover along the way. And Lord, once I do get started on my projects, may I trust that You have my very best interests at heart, whatever the outcome…even if it's not what I expected.

Amen

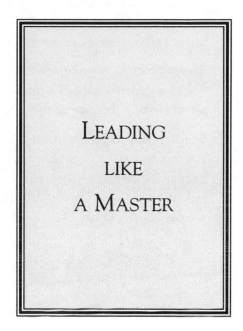

LEADING LIKE A MASTER

WHAT DOES IT TAKE TO LEAD LIKE JESUS?

I am frequently asked this question in a variety of different ways because I am a follower of Jesus and a leader. Let me share with you seven ways I believe we can model our leadership after Jesus—and practice the principles that He lived out.

Be Humble. Jesus used a model of servant leadership that was based on humility. Leaders following this would not exalt their own life or leadership.

Follow. To lead like Jesus, you must learn to be a follower. Just as Jesus turned to His Heavenly Father, Christian leaders should be seeking to follow Jesus rather than seeking after the next position.

Give Up. Christ-following leaders take pleasure in serving others. They give up personal rights. What better example than Christ Himself who left His position in heave to live as a human being?

Risk. As leaders following this model we can risk, because our trust is ultimately in God and His control of our lives. Think about how

Jesus approached Jerusalem at the end of His life. Despite the warnings of others, He faced the impending danger because He knew well the calling of the Father.

Serve. Practice humble service. When Jesus wanted to serve his disciples, he took a bowl with a towel and washed their feet. How might we be able to serve those on our team in a humble manner?

Share. Share responsibility and authority. Jesus consistently shared His power with those working with Him. Our ability to equip and instruct others encourages their responsibility and authority for the task at hand. Most importantly, pray for them, knowing that there are great needs in their families and in their individual lives.

Build. Build a team. I love the fact that Jesus worked with 12 disciples, and from those 12 the Christian Church was formed. You can multiply your leadership by empowering others to lead with you.

"For even the Son of Man did not come to be served, but to serve, and to give his life as a ransom for many."
(Mark 10:45, NIV)

Loving and gracious God,

As a leader and in my leadership I acknowledge You as the giver of all good gifts. I come into this day and week seeking Your wisdom, guidance, courage and strength. I want to lead more like Jesus, so I ask that You be with me in my deliberations. Help me to be wise in the decisions that need to be made for the sake of all those who have placed their trust and confidence in my leadership. May they see Jesus in me this week.

Give me insight to lead with integrity, that my decisions may reflect what is right and good. Keep me from shortsightedness and small-mindedness. Help me make decisions that are good for all my coworkers and those we serve. Guard me from being blindsided or seduced by self-interest. May I keep my eye on the bigger picture— Your picture—for our organization. Finally, dear Lord, grant me the humility to seek Your will in all that I do and say. I want all the glory be to Yours, O God, now and forever.

Amen

STICKTOITIVENESS

IN ORDER TO ACHIEVE GREAT THINGS, LEADERS WILL ALWAYS BE CALLED ON TO persevere. When all is said and done, this valuable, yet elusive trait commonly referred to as "sticktoitiveness" is a definitive characteristic of a leader.

There are certain seasons when Christian leaders and pastors are particularly tempted to give up. Some of these times include:

Financial downturns. Financial pressures often put leaders through the wringer leaving them strung out and weary. When their organization or ministry is struggling financially many leaders will take it personally.

Building projects. Many Christian leaders "expire" after the completion of a building project. The raising of capital and construction disruptions lull leaders into feeling as if they are no longer ministering, or they may collapse due to exhaustion.

Adding additional staff. Leaders work hard to add additional staff and tend to underestimate the amount of leadership and security it requires to work with others.

Periods of significant growth. Often growth pushes us into the next level of leadership, but not all are equipped to handle the new challenges of leading differently.

Periods following a pattern of people leaving. This can be congregants leaving a church, or even staff members. There is an emotional toll extracted with every departure, and it often means that the leader's workload will increase.

Heavy seasons of need. Every Christian leader goes through seasons when those around them, or they themselves, experience intense need. It may be due to illness, a leadership division, leadership failures, and family or health issues.

So, to you leaders who are just hanging on right now. God will reward your faithfulness and speak to you during this time. He often gets our attention about internal matters during this season. He may also want to teach you new things, including the value of persevering.

"But as for you, be strong and do not give up,
for your work will be rewarded."
(2 Chronicles 15:7, NIV)

Lord,

This role is tough at times and I need Your strength to keep going right now and in the days ahead. I thank You for Your sacrifice for me on the cross. When I think about the cross and ponder what You did for me, what You suffered and endured in Your life and leadership, I draw strength and power to face the daily grind of life.

During this season of challenge I need Your strength to lead in a manner that will bring glory to You. Please help me not to give up as I am tempted to do. Help me find Your strength to keep going. In Your presence, I find my purpose for leading even when I am weak. Those who follow me call me a leader. Help me as I try to live out my leadership role and faith—no matter what I must face. All these things I humbly pray in the name of my most blessed Lord Jesus Christ, my mighty God, and my ever-present Holy Spirit, upon whom I can rely.

Amen

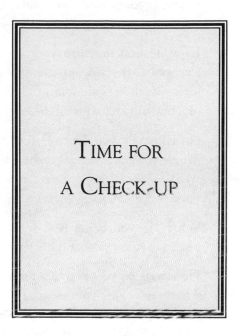

TIME FOR A CHECK-UP

HAVE YOU NOTICED THAT AS LEADERS, WE NEED TO SEEK OUT LEARNING opportunities—learning not just in our own work, but from those who work around us? For example, we need to watch and listen for learning opportunities in meetings—one of the places leaders spend (and sometimes waste) the most time.

At our office here at Arrow, we have developed a simple tool to check in on people. We start a meeting by everybody taking a minute to check in with what they are thinking and how they are doing. Over time, as trust and safety develop, people start to share ideas and feelings, which help the team to understand each other's concerns, problems and hopes.

The simplicity of this is that you are just asking questions. It is the best way to learn. So let me share with you a few starter questions for diagnosing the strengths and weaknesses of your organizational leadership. It is my way of checking in with you:

What are your unifying values? Do you understand the history of your organization and how your values have been demonstrated over time? The ability to provide context and meaning for the work people do is key. We have just undergone a review of our values at

Arrow Leadership and are using these value statements as a guide for our staff development days.

How do you organize your time? Is it spent on what you say is important? If you want to know if someone is really adding value, look at their calendar. Behavior does not lie, as our team psychologist shared with me.

On whom do you depend? Your real work team is made up of those people you count on to get the job done. This would include support staff, suppliers, users, direct reports, even government regulators. Your performance depends on the quality of those relationships.

What are you being paid for? All leaders must understand what results they are accountable for.

How well do you practice teamwork, empowerment, service and whatever values you espouse? Credibility is the number one issue for leaders. By taking an honest look at your own practices and asking others to look at them, you'll know better where you stand.

How do you convey difficult issues? By definition, learning requires an acceptance that one does not have all the answers. Your ability to discuss complex problems and develop solutions without making others defensive is a key to leadership and learning.

Why not consider using some of these questions with your colleagues or perhaps to create a staff team day together? Seek the Lord and listen to others for true wisdom in how to give leadership this week and beyond.

> *"But true wisdom and power are found in God;*
> *counsel and understanding are his."*
> (Job 12:13, NLT)

Father,

Over time, You have given me knowledge and experience. But it feels like I often do not have all that I need to lead these people. So I pray You'll show me what I need to be learning today in order to lead well tomorrow. Help me to understand how to use my leadership wisely and find a way to make the world a better place and further the work of Your kingdom here. Use my leadership to make life, with its problems, a bit easier to face.

Grant me faith, focus and courage and fill my days with purpose. Show me how I can serve You in the most effective way so that all of my education, knowledge and skill might find their true fulfillment as I learn to do Your will. As I go about this task of reflecting on who I am, how I spend my time, what I value, and those with whom I work in this calling, may I be ever aware that knowledge comes from learning and wisdom comes from You. Speak into my life with Your heavenly wisdom through books, family, friends and the experiences of the coming week.

Amen

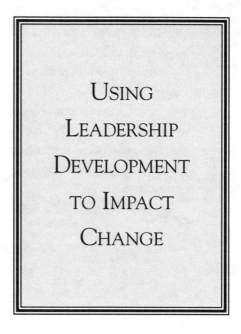

USING LEADERSHIP DEVELOPMENT TO IMPACT CHANGE

I AM SURE YOU ARE AWARE THAT THE ORGANIZATION YOU ARE LEADING IS undergoing change. Actually, let me take that back, for there are leaders who do not recognize that things are changing around them.

No, wait, let me take that back, too. I think most leaders know that things are changing around them—they just don't do much proactively to healthily adjust to and positively impact change. Is that you?

To prepare for successful change now and in the future, everyone must develop the capacities to lead and implement change.

Outstanding leaders play a vital role in helping organizations build commitment and overcome resistance. Leadership development, at all levels, can be the catalyst for building and sustaining the momentum for organizational change. Are you effectively developing the leaders that you work with?

If we as leaders can truly empower our staff and/or volunteer teams, they will help the organization redesign itself. Now if we really want to do this we must empower change-oriented leaders by helping them build capacity in four areas:

Commitment. Do they experience work as meaningful? Do they have a sense of where they are going and feel involved? Are they motivated?

Control. Do your staff leaders feel free to take action and do what must be done? Are they empowered to do their jobs well?

Challenge. Is your leadership team open to learning, or do they just like their ideas? Do they view change as an opportunity to develop skills and learn?

Connection. Do your team members know they can count on each other for help and support?

Things are changing rapidly. You and I, as leaders, need all the help we can get from our key team members. We cannot do this alone.

Dietrich Bonhoeffer offers us this prayer, which is not a bad way for you and me to start our day:

> O Lord, early in the morning
> My thoughts cry out to you.
> Help me to pray.
> I cannot do this alone.

One of the greatest leadership moves you and I can make is seeing that we intentionally develop the leaders around us. They are the ones who will be able to lead through the change and into the future.

**"He changes times and seasons; he sets up kings and deposes them.
He gives wisdom to the wise and knowledge to the discerning."**
(Daniel 2:21, NIV)

Lord Jesus,

While on earth You had many close and devoted friends, such as John, Lazarus, Martha and Mary. You built them up and breathed life into their lives. In this way you demonstrated that working with others is one of life's great blessings.

Thank You for the men and women that You have given me to lead and who love me in spite of my failures and weaknesses. I want to be the kind of leader who enriches the lives of those I work with, after Your example. Squelch my pride and allow me to learn never to look down on them. Let me behave toward them as You behaved toward Your friends and all those who followed Your leadership. Make me the kind of leader that is always watching for new leaders and helping them to develop to be all that they can be. May my team gain sufficient confidence and skill to guide this work into the future, knowing what it means to serve You.

Lord, I realize that as soon as I am no longer in this leadership position You will raise up another in my place. May I be part of that work starting today. Bind our team close together in You and enable us to help one another on our earthly journey and mission.

Amen

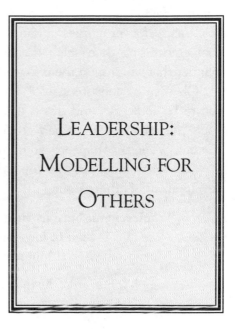

LEADERSHIP: MODELLING FOR OTHERS

THIS IS ABOUT THE NEED FOR LEADERS TO BE PROACTIVE ABOUT MODELLING. Too often, we get so busy that we do not invest in those around us. However, as a leader, this comes with the territory; we are models to those around us. When was the last time you encouraged someone to watch what you do in a specific area and then talked through how they might imitate you?

I want to encourage you to identify specific people and what you would like to model for them—and how you will do it. This may include your children, someone you work with, an emerging leader or those you mentor. What about taking someone with you every time you speak to or train others? Look for opportunities to model.

When you allow people to get up close, you will see the incredible power of modelling. Jesus liked hanging out with the disciples and wanted them to be with Him. But being close to people also requires that you are authentic in the relationship. If we want to be effective models, we must get close and personal.

To be an effective model, be sure that you allow others to know the "why" behind what you are doing. It is not enough to just have them watch. Take a few minutes to explain why you are choosing the approach you are taking. When you stop to explain, it multiplies the power of modelling one hundred fold.

Watch for principles around your areas of greatest passion and competence and then share these with emerging leaders in a winsome manner that will inspire them to lead in a similar way.

Oh yes…be consistent, too! The up and coming generation longs for you to be authentic, and this is measured by your behavior over the long haul. You don't have to be perfect. You are a model even in the areas where you fail. When that happens, admit it and talk about it.

Let's view modelling as top priority and be intentional about the development of others around us.

> **"Whatever you have learned or received or heard from me,**
> **or seen in me—put it into practice."**
> (Philippians 4:9, NIV)

Prayer of St Francis of Assisi

Lord,

Make me an instrument of Your peace.
Where there is hatred, let me sow love;
where there is injury, pardon;
where there is doubt, faith;
where there is despair, hope;
where there is darkness, light; and where there is sadness, joy.
O Divine Master, grant that I may not so much seek to be consoled
as to console;
to be understood as to understand; to be loved as to love.
For it is in giving that we receive;
it is in pardoning that we are pardoned;
and it is in dying that we are born to eternal life.

Amen

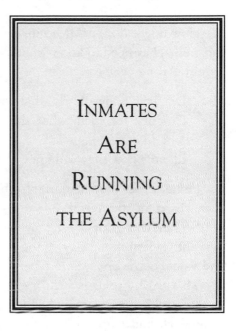

INMATES ARE RUNNING THE ASYLUM

WHENEVER LEADERS HEAR ABOUT THE CONCEPT OF SERVANT LEADERSHIP there are always some who struggle with it. Ken Blanchard ran into a manager who said, "If I become a servant to my employees, they're going to run all over me—the inmates will be running the asylum." Ken replied, "The truth is, the inmates are already running the asylum!"

As leaders, we can only be in one place at any given time. To lead by telling every single staff person what they should be doing at each moment of the day would be impossible! So, in reality, with the exception of the few times you are right there with them, they really are running the organization.

There is usually a season in our work, often in the summer months, when some responsibilities temporarily change due to staff being away. Take a look around you during those seasons and recognize those who picked up new responsibilities and are handling them well. Assess how well your team did running "your" organization.

I think leaders are best defined by looking at what their people are doing when they are not around. How well are they running the organization? Are they able to continue well on their own? The answer to that question actually comes back on us! Great leaders help their team run the asylum well!

How do we do that? It begins by helping them know what it means to run well. They need to know what a well-run organization looks like. Here are three things you can do:

> Let them know clearly what you want them to accomplish.
> Describe for them what the end result of their efforts will look like.
> Identify how they will know if they are hitting the target.

Perhaps your most important job as a leader is to provide this kind of clear vision for your team!

Servant leadership doesn't mean that employees do whatever they want. Servant leadership means helping your people live according to the vision and values of the organization.

This is why Jesus is such a good model. In His earthly ministry, He certainly did not go around telling people they could do whatever they wanted. He had definite rules for life! But He gave people His vision and His values for a life based on love and grace and then went about helping them understand how to experience it and put it into practice.

"When the Lord Jesus had finished talking with them, he was taken up into heaven and sat down in the place of honor at God's right hand. And the disciples went everywhere and preached."
(Mark 16:19,20, NLT)

Gracious Father,

You have given me the privilege of leading very capable people. They are committed to the cause and work hard. I pray that You will help me to see their highest potential and not miss the hidden skills that are waiting to be uncovered.

I know that I cannot do this work alone, but I confess that there are times when my personal pride gets in the way. Your scripture tells me that pride comes before a fall—and I certainly do not want that for myself or for this organization. Forgive me for the times when my pride has blinded me from the need to release people to new responsibilities. I pray, Lord, that I will never hold people back. I confess that feelings of insecurity so quickly cause me to mistrust.

May I find my security solely in You and then, in this freedom, lead in such a way that it frees other people as well. Ultimately, I realize that You are sovereign and in control, so I turn the leadership of this (ministry, business, organization) over to You. Lead in and through me for Your kingdom's sake.

Amen

STUDYING GREAT LEADERS

ONE OF THE MOST EFFECTIVE WAYS OF TAKING THE MYSTERY OUT OF leadership development is simply studying other great leaders. Find leaders in your field that are doing an excellent job and getting results; watch what they do and how they go about it.

Pretty simple, isn't it?

While it is an obvious way to grow, so many of the leaders I connect with fail to do it in a deliberate fashion. Instead, they keep grinding away in hopes that things will get better.

By observing others who are effective, we create a shortcut. Others can inspire us with what is possible and model how to pull it off. This is why mentoring is so important in the work we do with leaders.

The study of great leaders creates a benchmark for us. They set a new standard and inspire us to achieve higher potential.

Let me encourage you to intentionally seek out a leader you can learn from, but let me caution you. Be very discerning about who you are drawn to. Sometimes the best leaders to learn from are not the most inspiring speakers or motivating personalities—rather they are those who know how to execute and get things done. They are the ones that do things differently than you would and deliver better results. Do not be pulled in by the wrong leader—the person needs to have intellectual horsepower.

So let's start. Think of those you admire most and watch them carefully. Read what they have written. Analyze how they operate. Keep comparing their way of doing things to yours. Identify with their attitude and work habits and keep a listening ear for subtleties; they are often the real nuggets!

I have studied the Bible—scouring it for leadership inspiration—and have found Jesus to be the ultimate example of leadership. He has and continues to be the model that I strive to be led by, to lead like and to lead to.

Is your benchmark high enough?

> **"'Watch me,' he told them. 'Follow my lead.'"**
> (Judges 7:17, NIV)

Lord,

I know that I need to spend more time studying other leaders. But I'm not sure where to start! Will You make me aware of and guide me towards a person who portrays strong leadership skills? I want to study a leader that has the ability to motivate and influence—starting with themselves. I want to learn everything I can from another Christian leader who has practiced skills and established healthy habits.

You want me to grow as a leader. I know that, Lord. Help me to continuously pursue personal growth by gathering more information and skills. Guide me to study a leader that is both active and reflective. Someone who knows when to plan, think, study, ponder or take action.

There are different skills that I must grow in, some of which I may not even be aware of. May my study of another leader reveal the deprivations in my own life. May my study help me as a leader to be sensitive to the needs of those that I work alongside. Whether I am using a video, reading a book or studying another leader in action, give me eyes to see as a leader and learn everything I need to learn.

Amen

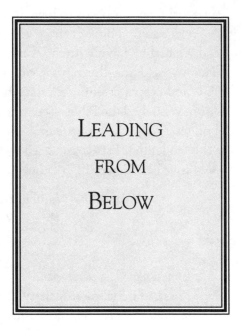

LEADING
FROM
BELOW

LET'S FACE IT—ALMOST EVERYONE HAS SOMEONE THEY REPORT TO, AND THIS relationship impacts us. A solid rapport with that person allows us to balance work and life more effectively, operate in a positive environment, and feel more fulfilled in our careers.

On the other hand, a poor relationship with our boss gives us a bad attitude—one that spills over into our personal lives when we are off the clock. In such cases, we often feel helpless, like victims to our careers.

Fortunately, there are things we can do to improve our relationship with our supervisors. We can begin by being better leaders. We don't have to be in charge or have a management position to be a leader. You can lead despite rank, title or tenure. Leadership is not about power or prestige. Leaders are those who take control of their lives to honour God and influence outcomes, which includes creating a more gratifying relationship with our bosses.

Here are four ideas to help do just that:

Do not take things personally. Your supervisor may irritate you, but he or she should not affect your disposition. As a leader, you can be confident about who you are and able to shrug off negativity before it weighs you down. Your supervisor's bad attitude may have nothing to do with you—so why take it personally? The less emotion you give to someone else's unpleasant nature, the more energy you have to spread some light on your way. You can also use your optimism to make your coworkers' days a little brighter. If you have a tough boss, chances are they also need some cheering up.

Be an example. Your words and actions set the tone for how you want to be treated. If you want more responsibility, prove yourself dependable. If you want loyalty, don't disparage your boss to your coworkers. If you want more pay, then justify your salary increase. Always hold yourself to a high professional standard, one that may even be higher than the one your boss holds. When you set a positive example, you contribute to creating a more positive, professional environment.

Earn respect, not praise. Your boss does not need another "best friend." Stop looking for affirmation from your boss and start striving for respect. This is earned by your hard work and integrity. You may never have the perfect relationship with your boss, but if you have his or her respect, then you are in a great position to influence outcomes.

Communicate. If you feel your boss's attitude has become a roadblock, have the courage to voice your concerns. Confrontation can be difficult, but it's easier than suffering through a bad situation. Approach your boss with tact; choose your words carefully to ensure your message is received clearly. Always have proposed solutions ready when you plan to highlight a problem. You may be surprised how quickly your situation can improve.

If you are leading from the second seat, stop acting like a victim and start leading. You can regain control of your professional life, and that will allow you to develop and maintain a positive relationship with your boss. You cannot force anyone to change, yet by being a leader you can influence professional behavior through your solid example. Each step you take towards becoming a stronger leader brings greater job satisfaction.

As you hone your leadership abilities, you become a person that others will want to promote. This professional progress will allow you to have an even greater influence over your environment in the future.

> *"Show proper respect to everyone: Love the brotherhood of believers, fear God, honor the king."*
> (1 Peter 2:17, NIV)

Dear God,

Help me to be the kind of leader that focuses on influence, not control. Leadership, the kind of leadership that You modelled in the life of Jesus, is not about position or authority. It's about influence and responsibility.

In the relationships where I am leading from below, help me to remember that my primary function is that of providing influence. Forgive me for the times when I have simply rolled over and not acted as a leader. Instead, allow me to hear and communicate to my board and the overseers the information that they need in order to think about the overall good for the organization.

Help me to improve my listening skills more than I talk. Give me wisdom to ask questions that will help broaden people's perspective instead of telling them how to think or what to do. May my leadership reflect the heart and actions of a helpful servant.

Amen

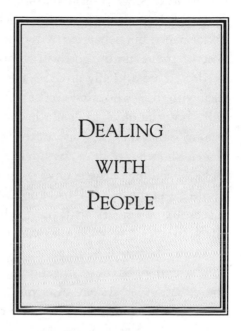

DEALING WITH PEOPLE

IMAGINE A LYRICAL VOICE AS YOU READ THIS IRISH TOAST:

> *Here's to you and yours and to mine and ours,*
> *And if mine and ours ever come across you and yours,*
> *I hope you and yours will do as much for mine and ours,*
> *As mine and ours have done for you and yours!*

Sounds like an Irish attempt at the "golden rule" and stands as a reminder of how we might treat others.

Not all systems and structures can relieve a leader from dealing with people difficulties. We have to meet, contend with and resolve all sorts of crises, from personality tantrums to someone who forgets a vital step in a process and holds up production.

While being firm in our pursuit of efficiency, leaders need to be thoughtful, tactful and careful. It would be easy to become carried away in the pressure of reaching a goal to the point of neglecting the people involved, like an elephant stepping on an ant hill and destroying it without thinking of the absolute havoc wrought among the ants.

As leaders, we achieve nothing on our own. Leadership brings out the best qualities and efforts of others. This complex operation of improving the performance and behaviour of the team around us requires that leaders must deserve and retain the goodwill of those around them.

If you are a highly driven leader, try being magnanimous for a while. Bear with those who are slower at picking up what you are laying down. Bear with those not quick to smell what you are cooking. Tolerate some mistakes as long as they do not go against the very heart of efficiency or values. When it seems hopeless to draw anything nearing perfection out of a worker, try to make something of them. Give them another chance.

Many of the best leaders I know rule by affection. If your organization is successful, you never apologize for having founded your progress on the affection of your people rather than on your dominance over them.

Now, there will be things that arise in dealing with people that need your attention, but don't forget to inquire whether something is wrong with the situation or system. Are you giving the person an opportunity to discharge their duty efficiently and effectively? Are they actually able to show the best that they can do?

> *"So in everything, do to others what you would have them do to you,*
> *for this sums up the Law and the Prophets."*
> (Matthew 7:12, NIV)

Prayer of Eusebius of Caesarea

May I be an enemy to no one and the friend of what abides eternally. May I not quarrel with those nearest me, and be reconciled quickly if I should. May I never plot evil against others, and if anyone plot evil against me, may I escape unharmed and without the need to hurt anyone else. May I love, seek and attain only what is good. May I desire happiness for all and harbour envy for none.

May I never find joy in the misfortune of one who has wronged me. May I never wait for the rebuke of others, but always rebuke myself until I make reparation. May I gain no victory that harms me or my opponent. May I reconcile friends who are mad at each other. May I, insofar as I can, give all necessary help to my friends and to all who are in need.

May I never fail a friend in trouble. May I be able to soften the pain of the grief stricken and give them comforting words. May I respect myself. May I always maintain control of my emotions. May I habituate myself to be gentle, and never angry with others because of circumstances. May I never discuss the wicked or what they have done, but know good people and follow in their footsteps.

Amen

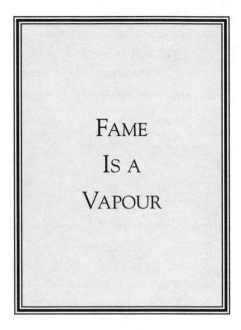

FAME IS A VAPOUR

Integrity—something that is precious, yet easily lost.

You see, nothing speaks louder or more powerfully than being a person of integrity. Absolutely nothing! Nothing stands the test like solid character. If you have it, then you can withstand any and all challenges you will experience as a leader.

Webster defines integrity as "the quality or state of being complete or undivided." A person with integrity is not guilty of hypocrisy (pretending or lying to other people) or duplicity (lying to ourselves and believing it). Leaders with integrity have nothing to hide and nothing to fear; they are an open book.

Integrity demands that you not only be truthful with others, but that you be truthful with yourself. We often lie to ourselves for our own peace of mind. We don't live up to our commitments, or look at ourselves with clarity. It may be easier, in the short term, to not face an unpleasant truth, but the truth catches up with us. For leaders, an attack on our integrity often results from ego needs. The ego desperately desires to be believed. Living with integrity means letting go of the need to prove our "rightness," especially to the detriment of others.

Living with integrity does not require perfection. Everyone is going to come up short of set goals from time to time. You will get angry. You will not meet your commitments. You will avoid. Integrity does not mean being free of mistakes; it means responding to those mistakes in a positive and courageous way.

Horace Greeley, an American newspaper editor during the 1850s, wrote, "Fame is a vapor, popularity an accident, and riches take wings. Only one thing endures and that is character." For Christian leaders, integrity keeps you standing against the intense challenges that our society will bring your way because Christ is at work in your spirit. Character will always win the day.

There is not a more effective defense for a leader than a life lived consistently and continually in integrity. It possesses incredible power to silence those who will come against you. My prayer for you is that you will maintain integrity and build on it. Don't allow the temptation of any short-term pleasure to rob you of this precious treasure.

"Love and truth form a good leader; sound leadership is founded on loving integrity."
(Proverbs 20:28, The Message)

Father,

Your word teaches me to do justly, to love mercy, and to walk humbly before You. Even when it brings about hurtful circumstances, help me to do the right thing in keeping with Your nature. May I not be found lacking in integrity, but rather be characterized by my integrity, which honours You.

With utmost confidence in Your power to heal and transform me, I come to You, seeking truth, integrity and wholeness. Help us, me as a leader and our entire team as an organization, to become who we say we are. May we be the women and men You have called us to be. We ask this in Your name, trusting in Your providence and goodness.

Amen

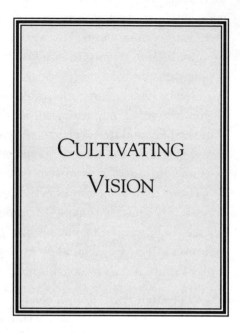

CULTIVATING VISION

HAVE YOU WRESTLED WITH THE CHALLENGE OF ONGOING VISION CASTING FOR your organization? Where does all this vision come from?

Vision "flows" when there is a convergence of three sources, much like three streams joining together to create a greater river:

Experience. God has allowed you to learn a great deal over the years. Out of what you have learned from the past there is a kernel of vision for the future.

Inspiration. God touches Christian leaders with an imaginative or spiritual spark, out of which comes a vision for the future. It does not have to be a "burning bush" experience, but there will be a definite God source to the vision that will inspire others.

Analysis. Often overlooked by Christian leaders, vision is frequently birthed out of some detailed review of data, trends and patterns. What has God already been up to in our midst—and should we not be following this in the future?

Within each of us leaders there is an energy and excitement that comes with vision. It gives you that jump-out-of-bed-and-get-to-work feeling. If you are not feeling very visionary or if your organization needs an infusion of vision, let me encourage you to pursue vision within these three areas and then use them as a means of telling the vision story.

And remember this: Vision is unique to every leader if it is cultivated out of experience, inspiration and analysis. If you borrow a vision you are simply managing another person's vision; you are not leading. To borrow a vision is to fail to lead. May you be filled with vision from God, inspiring you as a leader and your people, so that they will not perish.

"One night the Lord spoke to Paul in a vision, 'Do not be afraid; keep on speaking, do not be silent. For I am with you, and no one is going to attack and harm you, because I have many people in this city.'"
(Acts 18:9-10, NIV)

Disturb me, Lord, when I have become too complacent with what we are doing and where we are going. Disturb me when I am too well pleased with myself and our organization, when my visions to date have come true because I have dreamed too little and when I arrived safely because I have sailed too close to shore.

Disturb me, Lord, when the abundance of things possessed have caused me to lose my thirst for the water of life. Stir me, Lord, to dare to lead more boldly, to venture on wider seas, where storms will show Your mastery, where upon losing sight of land, we shall find what You intend for this ministry/organization over the curvature of the earth. I ask you to push back the horizons of my hopes and to push me into the future in strength, courage, hope and love.

Amen

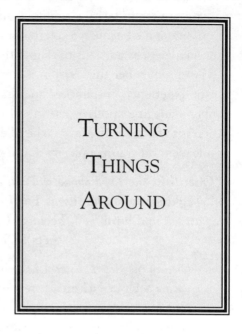

Turning Things Around

LEADERS OFTEN NEED TO BE ADEPT AT TURNING THINGS AROUND.

There can be turnaround situations, plans and procedures. But perhaps one of the more important abilities of leaders is our ability to turn our internal attitudes.

When a leader is being led by God, there is a heavenly ability to:

- Experience disappointment and see it as an opportunity to build character;
- Find yourself without clear answers and see it as a reminder of perseverance;
- Receive your success and use it as a foundation for a new level of thankfulness;
- Feel frightened about outcomes and use it to welcome courage;
- Be attacked by another and allow it to be the substance for longsuffering;
- Receive praise and allow it to be the composition of humility; Use pain as the fabric of endurance;

What keeps us from being able to able to navigate through the above circumstances?

Most often the answer is fatigue. When we are overtired there is simply not enough energy to engage in the process that initiates turnaround thinking.

Ask yourself, "How am I doing currently in turning things around these days? Am I overtired?"

Why don't you decide today to give yourself the gift of rest?

"Those who live according to the sinful nature have their minds set on what that nature desires; but those who live in accordance with the Spirit have their minds set on what the Spirit desires."
(Romans 8:5, NIV)

Gracious God,

You are the Lord of the Sabbath; teach me how to rest from my work. I need to be still and know that You are God. In the shadow of Your wings I long to take refuge. You are my strong tower against the enemy. In You alone is rest for my soul. You are my rock and my safety, my stronghold so that I can stand unshaken. You have always been my help. My heart clings to You and Your right hand supports me.

Sometimes, Lord, as a leader I find emptiness leaves me in a quiet stupor. I yearn to be inspired, lifted up and able to see beyond my present dryness. There are times it feels like I exist with very little communion with You. Yet, in the deepest part of me, something is stirring. I yearn for time with You, a time of rest.

When I read in Your word of Jesus calling His disciples and saying, "Come rest for a while," I sigh, longing for You to say those words to me today.

So, today, I will find my rest in You. Make my dry bones dance once again.

Amen

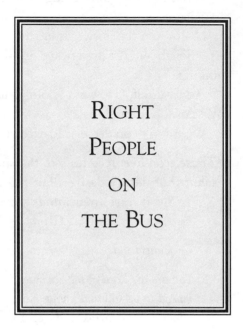

RIGHT PEOPLE ON THE BUS

MOST LEADERS I KNOW HAVE ALREADY READ *GOOD TO GREAT* BY JIM COLLINS. I frequently hear his maxim quoted about "getting the right people on the bus." He is referring to how important it is to have the right staff doing the right things on your team.

We all nod our heads in agreement. However, trying to discern who those right people are is another matter. Many leaders are too busy to even stop to figure it out; so let me encourage you to do a quick evaluation.

Let me share with you three different types of people we need on our team to accomplish the mission and to make our work together tolerable and fun:

Influencers. These are leaders who are able to get others excited about ideas and vision. They have a "sales" aspect to them and are responsible for seeing the fuel for the organization coming into the pipeline. We need influencers around to convince and motivate the doubters that a mission much bigger than any individual's scope can be accomplished together.

Contributors. These are the team members you can count on to get the work done. They deliver! They execute plans and don't spin their tires talking about it or get paralyzed by lack of organization. They are motivated by making a difference and touching lives.

Managers. People who are highly gifted at creating systems, structures and processes so that contributors have exactly what they need to be successful. Managers are excellent coordinators, planners and troubleshooters.

As you think about your team members, can you identify which group you would put them in? Make a pie chart divided into these three categories and write the names of your staff in the categories. Do you have too many of one type? Is one type absent altogether? Are you filling all of the roles yourself?

Ideally, we will have each of these groups represented on each team we lead, with a proper distribution of labour between them.

Is it maybe time for a mid-course correction and realignment of staff duties?

"Moses listened to his father-in-law and did everything he said. He chose capable men from all Israel and made them leaders of the people, officials over thousands, hundreds, fifties and tens. They served as judges for the people at all times. The difficult cases they brought to Moses, but the simple ones they decided themselves."
(Exodus 18:24-26, NIV)

Heavenly Father,

One of the toughest aspects of leading is finding and keeping great staff. I am turning to You to seek Your divine help and guidance as I examine all those who work with me now. Help me discern if they are all in a suitable place or position in their employment. I need Your wisdom to guide my footsteps on this path and lead me to find the proper things to say and do in this quest of managing team members well.

I desire that each team member use the gifts and talents You have given them. Where we have gaps, I pray, Lord, that You will attract great men and women who have a clear vision of Your standards and who believe in how we are trying to lead for Your kingdom's sake. May our team get the big picture, be fulfilled, have fun and feel the signature of Your peace in their lives through working together here. Grant this through Christ, my Lord.

Amen

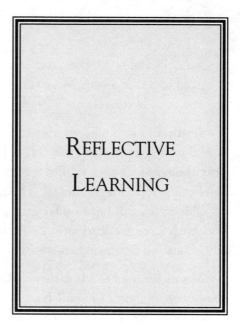

REFLECTIVE LEARNING

IN THE HUSTLE AND BUSTLE OF DAILY LIFE, MOST THINGS PASS US BY WITHOUT sticking. We experience a lot, but we learn relatively little.

Think back to the last conversation you had. Assume that you can remember some of what the other person said. Now, let me ask you, what did you learn? Probably very little. Often, the instant a conversation is over, our minds close the door and move onto something else.

Much of what happens in life and in an organization provides opportunity for us to learn. If, as leaders, we train ourselves to stop and ask the question "What have we learned?" we would be able to use the new information and insights more effectively. Then, if we leveraged what we learned by sharing it with others within the organization, we would all grow and the impact would be immense.

Very few organizations can be called learning organizations, simply because they are not "reflecting" organizations. Busyness rules. There is too much to do. People have no time to pause and think about what just happened. They rush frantically from one task to the next. The problem gets worse when there is financial pressure or a lack of adequate staffing. Yet, this is precisely when organizations need to use their learning well.

In the northern hemisphere, the summer months of July and August are usually times for a vacation. During time away, leaders often find reflection moments in the quiet gaps when enjoying recreation. While you do not want to be dragged back into work mode, try not to let the learning escape you when you are on your vacation. Take a moment to journal your thoughts and then review them when you return to the office.

Without reflection, change often gets messy. At best, people do new things without being convinced of the "why" and feel uncertain that they are functioning well under the new rules. At worst, they will sabotage the process.

Make reflection a regular practice for your organization or company. Allow time for it to happen, and make it deliberate. Build time for it in meetings and during review times with staff.

When you reflect, be sure that you focus on what worked well *and* what did not work well. Remember the positive experiences *and* the negative ones. You never know where your next great idea is going to come from.

> **"Let the wise listen and add to their learning,**
> **and let the discerning get guidance."**
> (Proverbs 1:5, NIV)

Lord,

I want to be a lifelong learner but I often turn off that learning opportunity when I'm busy on a vacation. Yet, don't allow my learning to consume me to the point where I ignore loved ones around me or fail to enjoy the moment. Please teach me. Let me hear You speaking creativity into me at all sorts of different times. May I become more seasoned at allowing reflection to be part of my life.

Humble me, Lord, so that I might learn from all those around me. Allow me to observe my family, my friends, the clerk in the store serving me. Help me to be curious and to ask lots of questions, but at the same time, guard me from my tendency to pre-judge how a particular type of learning is supposed to fit into my life. May I be open to new horizons that You want to show me.

You often taught Your disciples through the use of parables. Allow my life to be a living parable. Help me to see Your greater purpose through circumstances and experiences that I can then leverage to help others and be a better leader.

Amen

WHEN THINGS DON'T WORK!

WHAT DO YOU DO WHEN THINGS DO NOT WORK OUT THE WAY YOU IMAGINED? When some event or interaction throws us off balance, most leaders tend to react by trying to fix it. The better approach is to step back and arrive at a fully orbed solution.

First Step—Back to Strategy: The first step is to understand how this event impacts your overall strategy. Most ministries or businesses have some idea of what they want to achieve and where they want to be. If your organization has a formal strategic plan, looking at the event in light of this document is critical to determine how it will impact your goal attainment. If a formal plan does not exist, a much more focused meeting on strategy is imperative.

Second Step—Understand Your Limitations: Once the organization is agreed on what needs to be done to keep on track with its strategy, a detailed plan must be laid out. In this plan, the organization must be honest with itself. What can it do alone? Where is it going to need help? Will additional resources be required? The goal here is to know what you have, what you do not have, and how you will get what you need.

Third Step—Focus on the Solution: With the plan in place, execution is critical. This is where most organizations fail. Choices and sacrifices have to be made to achieve worthy goals. The tendency at this point is to micro-manage operations. Remember that things like tightening up on expenses, upgrading computers, hiring staff and downsizing the administration are not solutions but rather steps in a plan to achieve the goal.

Fourth Step—Measure and Corroborate: How will you be able to tell when the trouble has passed? Executing the plan is not enough. The organization needs to measure the impact of this plan and validate these measures against the overall goal. Regular monitoring is critical to ensure that what was implemented is delivering as intended.

While no leader likes to plan for the negative, we need to be honest with ourselves. Unpleasant things do and will happen. The successful organization will be one that understands this and develops a value of action rather than reaction.

> *"Since ancient times no one has heard, no ear has perceived,*
> *no eye has seen any God besides you,*
> *who acts on behalf of those who wait for him."*
> (Isaiah 64:4, NIV)

Lord God,

It is hard to really, truly let go of how worried and frustrated I can become when things do not go the way I planned. Why do I find it so hard, God, to allow You to handle what is troubling me? I seem to come to You over and over again with the prayer for the strength to "let go and let God," yet I think my problem is that I seldom do let go.

Help me to use the wisdom that You have given me, as a leader, to take the right steps. I know that Your wisdom will help to carry us through troubled times, and that eventually, we will emerge on the other side. I thank You for this in advance. I know You don't need my help. You simply want me to draw near and ask You for help. That is what I'm doing today.

I live in a world of such uncertainty. There are so many issues that weigh upon me and cause me to worry. But this is not the first time

I have faced trials, nor will it be the last. It is in Your word that we need not worry. So, I release my worries and my concerns unto you. I will use my God-given strengths and talents to do the best that I can and see to Your wisdom for guidance. Thank You for caring for me and for the people I lead. In Your precious name I pray.

Amen

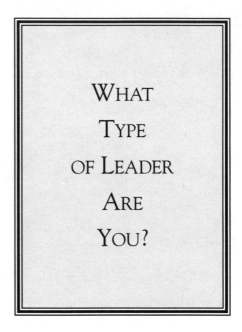

WHAT TYPE OF LEADER ARE YOU?

EVERYONE KNOWS THAT THE WORLD IS MADE UP OF MANY DIFFERENT TYPES OF people. This means our world is full of different types of leaders as well.

It is important to know what kind of leader you are, so you will know how to capitalize on your strengths, delegate effectively and educate yourself on how to lead better in a situation with less effort.

Perhaps this is why many leaders are struggling, challenged, overworked and exhausted. Most leaders spend an enormous amount of energy trying to do everything really well, yet lack the insight or resources to integrate more effective leadership skills.

When mentoring Arrow leaders, we assess what type of leadership style they default to. The best leaders are able to switch styles given various situations. However, we all have a default style we function in most comfortably. At all times (good or bad), the leadership style you choose is dependent on a number of situational factors.

The original work of Dr. Paul Hershey and Dr. Ken Blanchard at the Center for Leadership Studies identified four possible descriptions of a leader's style:

Directing. Directing leaders define the roles and tasks of the "follower," then supervise them closely. Decisions are made by the leader and announced, so communication is largely one-way.

Coaching/Selling. Coaching leaders still define roles and tasks, but seeks ideas and suggestions from the follower. Decisions remain the leader's prerogative, but communication is much more two-way.

Supporting/Participating. Supporting leaders pass day-to-day decisions, such as task allocation and processes, to the follower. The leader facilitates and takes part in decisions, but control is with the follower. This type of leader provides support and facilitates problem-solving and decision-making through a joint approach, to support and develop the followers' confidence in their abilities.

Delegating. Delegating leaders are still involved in decisions and problem solving, but control is with the follower. The follower decides when and how the leader will be involved.

Another style model by Daniel Goleman, author of *Emotional Intelligence*, identified six key leadership styles that he called:

Coercive. "Do What I Tell I You;" use in crisis mode for organizational turnarounds.

Authoritative. "Come with Me;" establish a new vision and culture.

Affiliate. "People Come First;" repair issues or motivate in crisis.

Democratic. "What Do You Think?" buy-in or consensus.

Pacesetting. "Do as I Do, Now;" quick results with a strong team.

Coaching. "Try This;" improve or develop employees over a long-term period.

The best of leaders use a combination of styles to obtain the desired results. Knowing what your core style is and how to use the other styles when necessary and with confidence will provide strong and powerful results.

The key concept in understanding your leadership style is to know how you operate naturally and what it is that makes you passionate about your work. Make sure that your role as a leader is aligned with your knowledge of yourself and who you are in Christ so you will gain strength, courage and inspiration (and motivate others to feel the same).

If you are trying to lead through a situation, and it is bogged down, then try changing your style. You may be surprised by how quickly people begin to support you.

> *"Whatever happens, conduct yourselves in a*
> *manner worthy of the gospel of Christ."*
> (Philippians 1:27, NIV)

Jesus,

My Lord, my King, my Savior, and my God. You walked on this earth and fully understand me. Please give me the strength to reject sin and the grace to remain pure through Your sacrifice for me. And now, as Your child and joint heir to Your kingdom, help me to be at peace with who I am. Give me the interest in fully understanding how You have created me—my gifts, my strengths, my personality. Allow my understanding of these things to shape how I function as a leader.

Jesus, I have offended You many times. Please forgive me. The more I understand myself, both the good things and those things I need to change, the closer I am drawn to You. Wash away my iniquities; cleanse me from my sin; purify me; protect me. Fill me with Your spirit and remake me so that as I lead, others will experience You through me.

Reign in my heart with Your power, wisdom, love, peace, grace, purity, mercy, glory and joy.

Amen

DON'T COURT DISASTER

WITH THE EXCEPTION OF NAVIGATING THROUGH A CRISIS, THE FIRST TASK OF any leader is to make the current business (or ministry) work. If that does not happen, there will not likely be an organization for you to lead. The second task we have as leaders is to reinvent the business. To get these two activities reversed is to court disaster.

Many times, leaders get distracted by the appeal of reinventing when what is needed is wholehearted attention to the business at hand. I am the first to champion innovation. We must continually improve our services and products. Every team member must be encouraged to "find a better way, every day." Yet I watch many organizations get so caught up in new things that they lose touch with their *raison d'être* (reason for being).

Here are some questions that can help you focus your team on the "first things:"

> What are the basics that propel or drive this organization?
> Does everyone know what the basics are and why they matter?
> What are the consequences of us ignoring the basics or starving them of resources?
> How well do we do the basics right now?

What improvements or changes must we make immediately?
If we do nothing new in the next year, what will the consequences be?
If we really need to make radical changes, how will we manage the process?

Innovation and change can be very seductive. It should be high on your agenda, but never let any of your people forget the basics.

"My purpose is that they may be encouraged in heart and united in love, so that they may have the full riches of complete understanding, in order that they may know the mystery of God, namely, Christ, in whom are hidden all the treasures of wisdom and knowledge."
(Colossians 2:2,3, NIV)

Lord,

Often my leadership does not give my soul peace of mind. I have wasted both money and time pursuing new ideas that have not furthered our mission or given us a sense of purpose. I have laboured for that which does not satisfy and is in fact distracting to what I should be doing. I have done this organizationally and in my personal life.

As a leader this can be distracting and frustrating for those who work with me. Help me to understand the good in my curiosity and to pursue the best possible way of doing things. Protect me from the evil one who may be using these new ideas and pursuits to keep me from the very things that You desire me to be about.

Lord, grant me contentment to do the basics well and to accept what each day brings and give me serenity in my leadership. Prod me to use my wisdom when I need to say no to a new pursuit. Nothing else satisfies me but You.

Amen

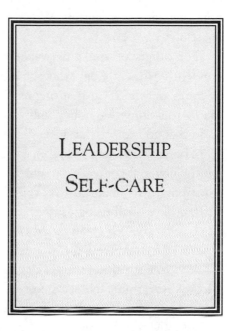

LEADERSHIP
SELF-CARE

IS YOUR LIFE FEELING LIKE ONE LONG WORKDAY AFTER ANOTHER? LET THIS BE a reminder to you that the most important part of your life and ministry is you. You are the sum of your parts, only one of which is work. The reason you are currently behaving the way you do is because it is comfortable. If you want to change the pattern, you have to disrupt your routine. This is a great time to do just that.

We have a hidden default switch somewhere inside us. The default is to spend ourselves on the needs of others—often at the expense of our own needs. Leaders everywhere struggle with this balance. It demonstrates a poor understanding of Jesus' commandment to "love your neighbor as yourself." If you don't love yourself, how are you ever going to love your neighbor? Why is it such a difficult task to love yourself? Why do we shy away from loving ourselves?

Many leaders have experienced personal crises. It may be the sudden death of a family member, a life threatening diagnosis for ourselves or a spouse, or perhaps the collapse of the organization. These types of situations alter us; we are not the same afterwards. These situations can bring about change at a very deep level. I have noticed that one of the gifts that flow out of personal crisis is the motivation to reevaluate life and to once again take note of what really matters. We find ourselves asking some really important questions.

For others of you, this wake-up call comes more in the form of an unrelenting inner thought that something is missing. It can happen as you pass by someone who is "just" sitting reading a book, sailing a boat, or engaged in some other enjoyable hobby, and you sense an inner longing for the freedom to do that and realize that you seldom seem to do the things you want to do.

The very first step in loving yourself is to realize you are unique, created out of love, for love. You are like no one else. You have a unique contribution to make to the world and you cannot realize your potential without first of all recognizing this uniqueness and all its implications.

Loving yourself means addressing weak areas that you know you have in a positive way. Make a list, if you have to, and set about finding a positive solution to each thing you dislike in yourself. Get a grip on reality—create a log of everything you eat, hours of sleep, times of recreation, reading, and intimate conversation. Write it down! It is too easy to cheat; make yourself accountable with someone who can make it fun! Create some precise goals and break them down over weeks.

Developing a loving attitude towards ourselves makes good sense. We need to let ourselves off the hook for not being perfect, celebrate our uniqueness, and be prepared to forgive and forget. When you love yourself, you set yourself free. You become free to enjoy and be interested in everything and everyone.

Make loving yourself a priority. Not only will you reap the benefits, but your neighbor will too.

"You must love the LORD your God with all your heart, all your soul, all your strength, and all your mind. And, 'Love your neighbor as yourself.'"
(Luke 10:27, NLT)

Lord,

You know how many times in the quietness of my thoughts and the deep recesses of my subconscious I believe lies about myself. I fail to see myself as You see me. Forgive me, Lord, and make my conscience alert to these moments so that I might rebuke wrong thinking and sense Your delight and pleasure in me as Your child, Your creation, Your leader.

It seems that I am often unmotivated to do this for myself—help me to change this. And Lord, I ask that You help me to see how my understanding of who I am in You affects those around me. I want to love my neighbor better, so show me how to love myself.

Amen

SETTING YOUR COURSE

I AM WRITING THIS FROM THE COCKPIT OF OUR SAILBOAT. ON THE SALON table I have laid out a chart where I have been plotting our course and waypoints for a journey to an island where we plan to anchor.

Every organization needs to work out an annual strategic plan. It is one of the responsibilities of a leader to see that the course is set organizationally for the coming year.

The two tasks above actually have a great deal in common. My navigational chart on the table is marked with pencil lines sketching a route that will guide our boat away from hazards and indicate the correct headings toward our destination. It is part of a strategic plan for our sailing journey.

Strategic planning for organizations is a systematic process we undertake as leaders. Through this process, we seek agreement and build commitment among our staff, constituents and key investors to establish priorities that are essential to our mission in response to the changing environment. A strategic plan creates a coordinated direction so that the organization can achieve its purpose.

The strategic planning process can be complex, challenging and even cumbersome at times, but it is an extremely powerful tool for leaders to achieve high-ceilinged goals for the organizations and the people we lead. In *Alice in Wonderland*, the Cheshire cat says to Alice, "If you don't know where you are going, any road will take you there." Out of our planning, goals emerge that guide our organization. Then, clear outcomes (waypoints) can be set for the journey.

An organization or church has a much greater chance of success if leaders have a strategic plan to guide the team towards the desired outcomes. If, on our holiday, we were to sail out of the marina without a plan, we may get in the vicinity of our island destination based purely on intuition and past experience, but then again, we may just end up sailing whatever direction the wind happens to blow. Being intentional and strategic will always accomplish more than simply being reactive and opportunistic.

Once you have developed four or five strategic initiatives or outcomes for your organization in the coming year and each member of the team understands the waypoints, you are ready to begin the voyage together for another year.

Why not take this month to review, pray and plan for the coming months?

"Surely the Sovereign LORD does nothing without revealing his plan to his servants the prophets."
(Amos 3:7, NIV)

Heavenly Father,

Help me as a leader to set direction. May it be Your direction for us as an organization. Guide me with Your vision for the future. Speak through my colleagues, our clients and our context. Help us to see the needs that we are uniquely qualified to meet.

You know me, Lord; I often want to get there in one movement. Help me to see the incremental steps or stages that will get us there without killing the crew along the way. Fill us with markers that show our forward progress, and make me aware of safe harbours where we might anchor during a storm.

Amen

HANGING ON

HAVE YOU EVER RECEIVED A GIFT THAT IS SO MEANINGFUL THAT IT SPEAKS into your life every time you look at it?

When we moved to Vancouver, some dear friends gave us a painting by Dan Sawatsky entitled "Hanging On." It features the roots of a fir tree grasping some thin soil and rocks beside a flowing stream on a gray morning. Every time I see this picture, I am reminded of what it means to persevere.

Leaders are always called on to persevere in order to achieve great things. When all is said and done, this valuable yet elusive trait is a definitive characteristic of a leader.

The world is full of those who "tried." After meeting with difficulty or rejections, they simply quit. They accepted failure and faded into the background. The worst part is that, in addition to quitting their organizations, they often quit on themselves. You cannot build leadership character on aspirations alone. Leaders are the ones who get up one more time than they have been knocked down.

Learning to ride a bicycle teaches us that failure only occurs when we stop trying. It is a lesson many leaders need to revisit. Why should succeeding at leadership be easier than learning to ride a bike? We will stumble at first—after all, it is only the mediocre that are always at their best. Ultimately, the leaders who persevere through the stumbling process learn enough to become successful. It's "staying with it" that separates the successful leaders from the wannabes.

Remember the words of Vince Lombardi, "We never lost a game, we just ran out of time." With this comment, Vince stretches out the timeline for us as leaders—something most of us do not do well. Leaders should begin to measure their success over time. Can you see the fruit of your leadership yet?

How are you persevering in God's vision for your life?

"You need to persevere so that when you have done the will of God, you will receive what he has promised."
(Hebrews 10:36, NIV)

Dear Jesus,

As I remember You persevering all the way to the cross for my sake, I am humbled by the things that cause my knees to buckle. I know You offer to me all the strength, wisdom, insight, power and relationships I need from the coffers of your bountiful resources. So forgive me the many times I have not asked for them and instead tried to forge ahead on my own.

Banish from my thought life the pressures that make me want to give up, and strengthen me for yet another day. Give me the grace to choose to persevere. Let me also have the wisdom to know when the pressure to give up is a sign that perhaps this was never Your idea in the first place. O Lord, make that clear to me. Would You encourage me this week with a word or a sign from You to keep on keeping on?

Amen

WHATEVER
HAPPENED TO…?

HAVE YOU EVER HAD A CONVERSATION ABOUT A SUCCESSFUL LEADER THAT you used to know but have lost track of? It often starts something like this, "Whatever happened to…?"

I am not sure what the percentage would be, but there are many "leaders" who are one hit wonders. They achieve a high degree of success within a particular organization or ministry. However, move them to a different organization and they just don't seem to cut it and eventually disappear. The leader found him or herself unable to replicate, to the same degree, their former success level. "What was I thinking?" is the common phrase heard at this moment!

For whatever reason, they landed in a position of leadership within their previous organization where there was an alignment of their calling and passion, and that of the organization. When these connect, success follows and the leader usually stays put for many years.

I met with a wonderful leader at a thriving church and was interested in knowing more about his leadership. I asked him, "What is it about your leadership that works?" He leaned back in his chair thinking, then he pulled his chair up close to the desk and leaned towards me and whispered, "I don't know."

Although embarrassed at not having a more robust answer—he was at least aware that he did not know. In fact, he knew much more than he realized. His leadership was responded to positively and obviously blessed, because of many positive leadership traits, such as trust, integrity and a clear understanding of his position in Christ.

The key to moving beyond a one-hit wonder is awareness. Self-awareness, both of who you are as an individual and as a child of God, is the core of great leadership. A self-aware leader is able to analyze why and how their leadership works in a particular setting and then extract the principles for application with different people in a wide variety of contexts.

I love being with leaders who have led very successfully in a number of settings. I consistently find that self-aware leaders have a deep understanding of their emotions, strengths, weaknesses and needs, and what guides them. They tend not to be overly critical, nor are they unrealistically hopeful. They are just honest with themselves and others.

Can you work on self-awareness? Yes, you can, but not by yourself! You need a wonderful mentor or counsellor to guide you to new depths of self-understanding. But the journey is worth the effort—for all of us.

"For you created my inmost being; you knit me together in my mother's womb. I praise you because I am fearfully and wonderfully made; your works are wonderful, I know that full well."
(Psalm 139:13-14, NIV)

O Lord,

I am painfully aware that I avoid, and even fear, self-awareness. Jesus, I ask You to give me the grace to trust You in this. Give me the courage I need to face myself...the good, the bad and the ugly. Please direct a godly person my way, who can guide me into being more self-aware. Someone who has done, and continues to do, the hard work of self-examination before You.

Holy Spirit, show me how to be a more real, authentic and honest person and leader.

Amen

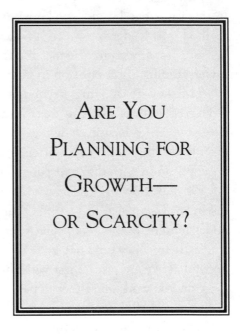

Are You Planning for Growth— or Scarcity?

As leaders, we eventually get engaged in the process of budgeting for the coming year or sometimes even the coming years. Let's look at this from the perspective of your local church for a moment.

As you prepare to do your next budget, pause to ask yourself, "Are we planning for growth—or scarcity?"

It costs more to grow a church or business than it does to maintain one. To remove barriers to growth, you need to increase funding for activity, specifically by budgeting for people. A growing organization must always hire staff ahead of growth. And that takes money!

The last few years have taken their toll on the confidence of most organizations. Why is this? I think that in many cases it is because they have veered away from the hard work of laying out a strategic plan that compels growth.

It also reflects a lack of faith—fear that resources are too scarce. Once a leader begins to lead out of fear, the end result is already decided and the organization limps along in a survival mentality.

When you begin to engage the process of preparing a budget for the coming year, it could begin with naming and facing any fears that still linger from the past, and then asking God to bring clarity to the desires He has for the future.

There are several considerations in the process:

- Prayerfully establish ministry goals for the following twelve months.
- Develop a strategic business plan consistent with your goals.
- Break down your overall goal into intermediate goals.
- Create administrative systems that support your ministry plan.
- Develop a vision-casting communications plan.
- Clarify what distinguishes your unique calling from everyone else.
- Decide in advance the markers that will gauge trends and then adjust accordingly.
- Identify new ministry opportunities.
- Develop an annual and monthly operating budget.
- Acquire and train team work habits and skills that boost effectiveness.
- Dare to risk for growth. If you will dream just one dream, you can realize many.

The outcome of the mission is too important to not plan diligently—and remember…

"We can make our plans, but the LORD determines our steps."
(Proverbs 16:9, NLT)

Dear Jesus,

Is there more that You want to do in and through us than I am planning for? Have I become snagged by fear from the experiences of the past year (or before) that keep me from taking a risk today? If so, I ask that You bring any that I need to be aware of to my attention. Help me to have a vision for what we could do if only…! Give me, in Your freedom, the ability to dream again…to dream God-sized dreams. Grant me wisdom and skill to both envision and walk out a plan to move forward in Your will.

Help me as I step into this planning mode to be more focused on the mission than the finances of how to get there. While I know that the managing of our resources is so important, I acknowledge that sometimes I spend too much time being concerned about the money and not enough about the mission. You are the God that owns the cattle on a thousand hills. Please show me how Your vision and dreams can be accomplished.

So free me, Lord, to pursue making an even greater impact for Your kingdom this coming year. I give You all the glory and praise for our accomplishments.

Amen

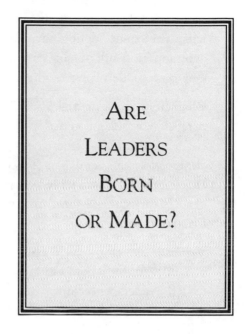

ARE
LEADERS
BORN
OR MADE?

ARE LEADERS BORN OR MADE?

Now, there's a long-standing debate! There are very interesting arguments on both sides.

That question has challenged society for centuries. However, countless deposed monarchs and hapless heirs who lost family fortunes stand as evidence that leadership is not genetic. I have witnessed God raising up leaders for their own generation. Yes, some people are born with traits favourable to good leadership, but overall, leadership tends to be drawn out, nurtured and developed.

In my work with emerging leaders, I find that some vital leadership characteristics can be cultivated, while others cannot. Leadership skills and traits conducive to development include: a heart for God, communication skills, personal growth, time management, focusing priorities, delegating, and making tough decisions.

However, other leadership traits or skills are not conducive to development growth. Recognize and be realistic about what can and cannot be easily improved so you don't exhaust yourself trying to repair areas that, even after enormous efforts are exerted, improve only imperceptibly. I would include in this list:

Vigor. This essential leadership trait is tough to instill. Unfortunately, leaders with low energy normally attract followers with the same deficiency. Related traits: drive, desire and determination, are tough, if not impossible, to teach effectively. You may get a sudden burst of adrenaline, but it rarely lasts.

Character. This essential leadership quality is more important than competence. Competence can be taught, but someone's basic character cannot be redesigned. There are no "three-day character clinics" you can send liars and cheats to for retrofitting. Lack of character brings down more leaders than any other trait of leadership. Leaders can succeed for a time without it, but eventually they are found out.

Vision. Developing, casting, communicating and gaining commitment for a bold vision is one of the first responsibilities of a leader. Leaders who cannot see past today and are more interested in maintaining than in growing their organization rarely inspire followers for long.

These listed traits should especially be considered when you are evaluating potential leaders for positions.

> *"Remember your leaders who taught you the word of God.*
> *Think of all the good that has come from their lives,*
> *and follow the example of their faith."*
> (Hebrews 13:7, NLT)

Gracious Father,

Thank You for the privilege of being a spiritual leader. I realize that with leadership comes responsibility. Lord, please give me what I need to lead well and responsibly. Thank You, Lord, for investing in me.

Thank You also for giving me the traits that cause others to want to follow me. My passion, vision and energy—these are things I acknowledge come from You. I praise You for giving me the ability to think, to handle relationships and to communicate vision. Thank You for my character and remind me, in whatever way needed, to guard and protect this cherished treasure. It can be lost in a moment of indiscretion or stupidity. I remember leaders where this has occurred. I pray for them and the people who have been hurt as a result of their behavior.

I also pray with a humble heart because I know that it is only by Your grace that my name is not listed among them. Keep me alert to the subtle things that erode character. May they be illuminated by Your heavenly light so that I recognize them clearly.

I lead into today knowing that born and made, I have a leadership responsibility that ultimately comes from You—not from my board, not from my career title, but from You as the Almighty God. May I lead in ways that cause others to praise You.

Amen

SEASONAL MENTORS

WHO IS MENTORING YOU RIGHT NOW?

If we are to continue to learn and grow as leaders, we need mentors who will encourage our growth. Maybe this is a good time for you to consider your mentoring needs.

One summer, we went sailing as a family and took a mentor with us—a sailor named Les with 38 years of experience. At the end of a week living in the close quarters of a sailboat, we all agreed that Les was a great relational match for our family. He also knew what we needed to learn and how to teach us to develop and enhance our abilities on the sea. He is a great example of a short-term mentor.

So, how do you select the right mentor for you and your growth areas?

The optimal mentor possesses the expertise, commitment and time to provide assistance. In locating potential mentors, an obvious starting place is the immediate environment—for instance, other leaders in your area.

There is no fixed rule about what traits or circumstances surrounding a given mentoring situation are the most critical. The most frequently mentioned characteristic of effective mentors is a willingness to nurture another person. If there is not openness, a willing spirit, or a desire to help another on the part of the mentor, then the process will never get off the ground.

It is also beneficial to seek mentors who are spiritually mature, people-oriented, flexible and empathetic. Add on social skills and qualities of receptiveness, responsiveness, openness and dependability and you have the makings of a great potential mentor.

The relational chemistry between the mentor and the protégé is at the heart of the mentoring process. One of the first things to be considered when establishing a mentoring relationship is proximity. In our work with Arrow leaders we have typically matched mentors and protégés using geographical proximity and relational chemistry as the main criteria. Although, let me be quick to add that administrative convenience should not be the only factor you use in making decisions about a mentoring relationship match. We have had some successful mentoring relationships built over distance with time—but not without occasional face-to-face meetings.

So, before this week draws to a close, take an hour to list the predominant leadership issues you expect to face in the next three months. Consider not only your leadership at work, but also within your family, community and church. Pick one or two from this list and deliberately choose to seek a mentor who can help you to grow through these next months.

> *"Plans fail for lack of counsel,*
> *but with many advisers they succeed."*
> (Proverbs 15:22, NIV)

Lord,

Help me to remember that I cannot, must not, try to lead by myself. Give me a teachable spirit and openness to seek the wisdom and counsel of godly men and women, realizing that this is Your work—not mine. I know that You often speak through others, so help me to seek them out and listen well.

Bring to mind the very people that can assist me with my current leadership challenges. And when I am with them, close my mouth and open my ears so that I might learn from them. We are all in this together for Your sake—and we need to assist and rely on others to *get the job done. Lord, help me to discern and recognize spiritual and humble, yet confident mentors who would be Your best choice for me during this season of life and leadership.*

Lord, may I also be willing to be there for others. Save me from feeling that I am too busy when someone asks for my help or wisdom. May I be a Paul to some Timothy or an Elizabeth to a Mary.

For Your name's sake,
Amen

CURE FOR THE SUMMERTIME BLUES

SOMETIMES THE MONTHS OF JULY AND AUGUST CAN LEAVE US WITH A SENSE of the summertime blues. We enjoy some time away for vacation time and when we return to work, it is just a little different than what we experience the rest of the year. People and staff can be away and sometimes we find it difficult to concentrate.

Here is a quick list of things you can do to help bring focus when you are drifting:

- Set goals
- Measure your successes
- Invest in going forward
- Set time aside daily for planning
- Encourage more dialog
- Listen more intently
- Be more concrete in your goal setting
- Plan monthly—write it down and review
- Help others achieve their goals
- Share publicly the passion and call
- Set your priorities based on the passion

- Set goals that actually support the priorities
- See vision as a process—always being sharpened
- Continue to develop your team
- Write out your personal vision
- Work on your organization's vision
- Develop a plan to communicate these visions
- Be honest with yourself first, then with others
- Help your family members to express their goals
- Respect other's ideas
- Set up your next leadership meeting to discuss plans
- Work on some "what if" scenarios
- Identify your true passion
- Create and share a list of goals and priorities
- Choose to respect others
- Reflect and be aware of both helpful and constraining forces
- Seek new experiences for growth
- Lead by example
- Make notes to follow through on ideas—don't lose them
- Acknowledge your own needs/desires
- Clarify your own intentions towards the organization
- State them clearly
- Spark dialog within both family and organization
- See the vision through
- Revise the mission/vision statement for the ministry
- Start developing a family vision statement
- Truly develop a clear vision/mission statement
- Hold each other accountable to that vision
- Work on your own personal vision statement
- Present a more positive attitude to the world
- Understand where negativity exists and minimize it
- Pray and pray and pray

Being a leader is tough—especially when you have to keep continuing through seasons like this. But the success of your leadership is largely based on your perseverance. Peter Drucker's recipe for success as a leader is: "Find a need that beats your drum. Create a plan, and then make a dent. Trust that your rewards will come. And credit them as heaven sent."

"'I know the plans I have for you,' says the LORD. 'They are plans for good and not for disaster, to give you a future and a hope.'"
(Jeremiah 29:11, NLT)

Lord,

I first enter seasons that are supposed to be restorative with excitement and grand hopes. But suddenly, I feel the exhaustion set in and I realize that I have been trying to do so much on my own strength. There are many ways I now see that I have not set healthy standards and my body and mind are paying for it. Lord, I ask Your spirit to guide me during this vacation season, back to the place You want me to be.

With people coming and going for their vacation, I confess that I drift in my thinking and am not always as productive as I could be. So, Father, call me back to Your vision. Help me learn to use my days and hours wisely while maintaining healthy boundaries. You are the one who gives me strength. Help me to choose well and to not force outcomes that You do not even expect. Help me hear and understand Your plan, I pray, in the Savior's name.

Amen

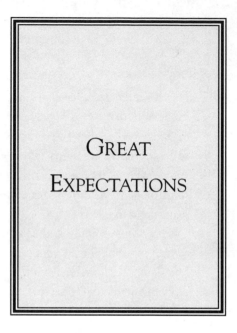

GREAT EXPECTATIONS

ALL LEADERS NEED REFLECTIVE SEASONS: TIME DEDICATED TO REST, regrouping and realignment, and time to review goals for the coming months. Here is a helpful exercise to create clarity of goals for your team and your leadership.

"What do I expect this person to do?" Write this question at the top of a blank piece of paper. Then, down the left-hand column, write the names of each of your key staff members, and answer for each specifically.

"What does the organization expect of me?" Write this question at the top of another piece of paper and distribute to each of your key staff members.

This quickly and effectively lays out roles and expectations. When a leader and his teammates can answer these questions completely and explicitly, they have come a long way toward solving the operational and interpersonal problems of the ministry or organization.

Effective leadership consists of striking a balance between the task and the relationship between activities and people. Leaders often find themselves at one end of this polarity. Either they are much more comfortable as a "task master" or as a "people person." The former has a reputation of burning through people in order to get things accomplished. The latter is often described as "great to work for" but "does not get the job done fast enough or with the capacity possible."

For Christian leaders, striving for this balance seems even harder. The people working on their team are highly valued and cared for. As a result, the leader can become conflicted when trying to find the balance between the relationship and getting the task accomplished. Clear communication and clarity of goals or expectations is the answer.

Setting out clear expectations has several advantages. It lays out the path where the organization is going. This helps people see the big picture and prevents them from being frustrated by only being able to see their area of work.

Having clear goals, even short-term goals, brings the members of the organization into alignment—all paddling in the same direction. The exercise I listed above provides an opportunity to see how perceptions differ.

Taking the time to set goals for individual team members gives them activities they can pursue on their own, allowing freedom for leadership responsibilities.

When a team member has a defined set of goals, he or she can fill their needs for both autonomy and challenge. These are two of the most sought-after aspects of rewarding employment.

Goals also give leadership a concrete means of measuring performance.

Goal setting, at its very best, is a collaborative effort—leader and team members working together to set goals that will meet the organization's objectives. There is something extremely fulfilling about being a part of establishing the organization's goals and objectives.

"If it is true that you look favorably on me, let me know your ways so I may understand you more fully and continue to enjoy your favor."
(Exodus 33:13, NLT)

Lord,

You are calling me to set wise direction and I need Your guidance to do so. My coworkers also need my guidance. Lord, we all need clarity, yet I confess that I often get so caught up in my own "to do" list that I neglect this leadership responsibility. Through Your mercy, may I practice my leadership through the lens of all of "team." Help me to care enough to seek great alignment with staff, volunteers...and even within my family.

As the leader, help me to build security and strength in our team by making sure we are all clear on our roles. If this requires a change from what we have been doing for the sake of our vision from You, then grant the grace for me to lead us toward that future, even when it means leaving some comfort and familiarity behind. Give us all the peace that comes from knowing what is expected and why.

Amen

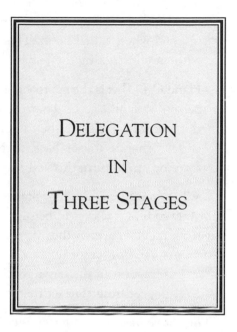

DELEGATION IN THREE STAGES

OVER THE YEARS, I HAVE PROBABLY TALKED TO LEADERS MORE ABOUT delegating than any other topic. Why? Because most of us are not very good at delegating.

Not everyone is ready to take on a fully delegated task, so here is a means to identify where your team members are at in these three stages. Then you can lead accordingly.

Hand Holding. New staff or untried people in your organization don't want to be thrown in over their heads and you probably would be a little uncomfortable letting them go unsupervised. Until you are both comfortable, try to be a partner in the task, participating in the decisions, checking along the way. Practice your best participatory style but remember the goal is to train them to carry the ball on their own.

Consulting. When you feel ready, let them go off on their own. Let them feel free to come to you whenever they need help or information. Often, I find that lacking information stops production, more than skill or competency. Use your coaching techniques here but choose to remain outside the task and only respond when called upon. This helps your people feel supported without constricting their style.

Hand Off. This is the approach when you feel really good about the person, they feel good about themselves, and you trust them to do the task well. Delegate the total responsibility and step aside. This is your chance to get back to the creative work you should be focusing on. In turn, this will reap great results for the organization.

When you are delegating, praise people whenever you can. Go out of your way to find a reason to be supportive and do it in a clear way. Telling our team members when they do a good job is one of the most important things you can do. Unfortunately, some leaders find praise difficult, while others just forget it in the busyness of their lives.

Nothing gets results faster than honest feedback and praise.

"They have been a wonderful encouragement to me, as they have been to you. You must show your appreciation to all who serve so well."
(1 Corinthians 16:18, NLT)

Dear Lord,

Whenever I think of You delegating to and empowering us as Your children to continue the work of Your kingdom, I am humbled. I know how often I fail You and stumble along, yet again and again You release me to follow your instruction. I also realize that You do not spell it all out for me. Yes, You give me boundaries and direction, but I have to figure so much out on my own. Help me to lead more like You by doing the same for my colleagues.

By Your mercy, keep my ego from getting in the way. I know that is usually what keeps me from sharing the load with others. Heighten my discernment so I am more quickly aware of when I should be delegating, and help me to remember the great need of praising and affirming for a job well done.

Amen

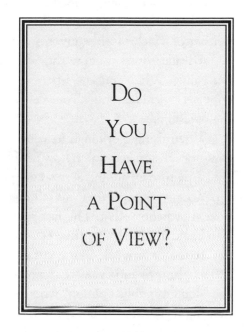

DO YOU HAVE A POINT OF VIEW?

THERE ARE MANY REASONS WHY LEADERS FAIL. AMONG THE MOST OBVIOUS are these:

- They make wrong assumptions.
- They make poor judgments based on incorrect or insufficient facts.
- They cannot get the resources they need.
- They fail to win the support and respect of those following them.
- They fail to manage the details and allow the controls to slip.
- Their execution is poor.
- They forget the priorities of character and integrity.

But there is another reason that perhaps exceeds all of these together. It impacts everything and everyone else around the leader. It is extremely costly and yet seldom gets much attention. The villain is the leader who has no clear focus.

Partly, this is about setting direction. People expect leaders to set direction and help them to know where to focus their efforts. But there is more.

Leaders need focus so they can explain "why." There is a noticeable glut of leaders who are adept at telling everyone the "what" and the "how"— neither of which inspires anyone.

A leader's focus is more than direction; it is also an expression of his or her values. When you say "I believe this is what we must do, because...," it conveys logical reasoning, your personal character, and that you reflected on the decision.

When things get tough in your setting and you are facing a significant challenge, listen and watch how people react. When the heat rises and ideas are being thrown around at random, people duck and dive and change their tune to suit whoever they are talking to. One minute they believe this, the next they believe that. The last person they talked to is where their latest idea came from. Because they lack clear focus they will defend anything.

Trying to arrive at your focus can be a tortuous process. You first allow ideas to surface and evaluate them as honestly as you can. You test them in the "court of public opinion" where others can challenge your thinking. Try floating a few trial balloons, and be willing to change your mind if you receive new information. This shows your willingness to listen and your flexibility. But a leader who constantly changes positions to please others, or to prove them wrong, is not leading.

At least that's my focus.

> *"Trust the LORD with all your heart and lean not on your*
> *own understanding; in all your ways acknowledge him,*
> *and he will make your paths straight."*
> (Proverbs 3:5-6, NIV)

Lord,

I realize that those who look to me as their leader want me to be focused. When I am not focused, it causes them to be confused, and I end up wasting a great deal of their time and energy. Help me to value focus more. Inspire me to be led more by You, so that I can be clear in our direction and precise in focus. You want to direct my paths, Lord, so stop me, please stop me when I stray.

Amen

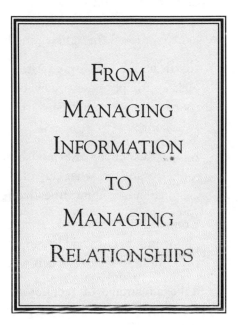

FROM
MANAGING
INFORMATION
TO
MANAGING
RELATIONSHIPS

IN JUST A SHORT PERIOD OF HISTORY, THE FACE OF LEADERSHIP HAS CHANGED profoundly. Leaders today live and function in a relationship economy. You face a complex matrix of challenges that leaders 20 or even 10 years ago could not have imagined.

You have to manage relationships with people from all over the globe. Technology has allowed us to communicate more easily with people and our Rolodex file of contacts has grown exponentially. Your organization's relationships with vendors, partners and clients or customers dot many places on the map. The end result is relational exhaustion that begins to erode some of our closest friendships.

If you want to stay ahead of this frenetic relationship game, there is something you need to know: Senior leaders can manage about 24 relationships well. How many relationships are you managing? How well are you doing?

Make a list of your most important relationships both personally and organizationally. Now take this list and identify the 24 most important relationships for you to manage—stating why they are important. Strive for a good representation of family, work, restorative relationships and those in which you are caring for others. This is a meaningful exercise and helps bring the importance of relationships and friendship back into focus. Here are some relational tips on keeping in touch with friends.

Just a phone call away. Although you may not have the time to pick up the phone every evening to call one or all of your friends, try to make a commitment to call each of them at least once every two months.

Keep a "Calendar of Friendship." Mark on it which friend you last spoke to and on what day of the month. Note each call on your calendar, and commit to calling each friend regularly.

Contact list. Be sure to keep your address book updated with current phone numbers and addresses, as it becomes more difficult and time consuming to keep in touch when you have old numbers.

Take advantage of technology. With the ever-growing world of social media, there are some great ways to keep in touch with friends right at your fingertips! Use them to send a spontaneous note, set up a lunch date or even plan a getaway with a group of friends.

Cards and notes. Even with this new technology at your disposal, don't forget that the handwritten word is still the best and most personal way to show that you care.

Small gifts. Often special occasions arise for your friends and you cannot always be there in person to celebrate. For times like these, sending a small gift in the mail is a great way to show that you care and that you wish you could be there.

Annual get together. Another great way to keep in touch with friends is planning an annual get together. Keep it at the same time of year so everyone becomes familiar with the trip or event. Usually, there is a circle of friends that remain acquainted as years pass, so spending time together annually keeps up the close connection.

"Greater love has no one than this,
that he lay down his life for his friends."
(John 15:13, NIV)

Here is to friendship!

Lord,

I know You love people and I know that this life You have called me to is not just about leadership—it is about people. It is all about people. Yet I get so caught up in leading that I sometimes forget about my friends or feel guilty when I do think of them. So help me, Lord, to be a better friend. Help me to make it a priority to stay in touch with friends and to place a high value on relationships. May my restoration from time spent with my friends be reflected right back into those around me. May You bless each one through me, Lord.

Amen

EXCHANGE
YOUR
WATCH
FOR A
COMPASS

ARE YOU THE TYPE OF LEADER WHO PLANS AHEAD? OR INSTEAD, DO YOU FIND yourself disorganized, chaotic and unsystematic—never making progress on your most important goals? What are your priorities?

Each leader I meet has a unique style. If what we have set before us is really important, we have to put some time into planning. Realistically, I know that I will not accomplish everything in my daily plans, but I find that I can sit down once a week to restate the important goals for the week ahead, and once a month to write out objectives. What works best for you? A summer planning marathon? Monthly planning times? Weekly updates or nightly reviews of what you got done that day and hope to accomplish the next?

Bobb Biehl taught Brenda and me the importance of annual planning. Now, each year between Christmas and New Year's, we put substantial time into planning for the 12 months to come. Since the family is involved in the process, it enables us to make sure that I am not travelling when I am needed at home. We also have traditions in our marriage, such as our anniversary or our annual time in the summer enjoying coastal cruising with friends. By stopping to consider these important things annually it enables us to live a somewhat balanced, though busy, life.

The change of the calendar year is an excellent time for us to plan for the next 12 months—personally, as a family and organizationally. In our ministry, we also gather as a core team to examine the "must dos" for the coming year, and then set some objectives for each month. This gives shape and purpose to the year ahead.

This is the time to take off your watch and pick up a compass, to re-identify your direction and those things that make up the best use of your hours, days and weeks. As leaders, we are usually driven by time and, therefore, try to control the use of each hour or minute in the day to maximize effectiveness. However, if we only plan our time and miss the direction, we can suddenly find ourselves having completed our schedule of events yet completely unsatisfied because we have sacrificed the things that matter most.

Many leaders admit to not taking the time to do this kind of "compass" planning. Why is that? It seems easier for them to make an appointment with someone else than it is for them to book a "compass time" appointment with themselves.

As leaders, we are often caught in this battle between those things that are good and those things that are best. When we take the time to plan with a compass we create an antidote for frantic living. As we lead out of the direction the compass gives, we can actually make changes to our schedule based on a renewed sense of knowing what to do and what not to do.

Let me make one more observation. There is a dark side to this preoccupation with time and "the watch." I've observed that leaders who like to control their time, money and things also tend to try to control people. They express more concern about efficiency than about calling, purpose or relationships, often short changing what is really important in life.

Remember, it is not about getting more things done—it is about getting the right things done.

"Teach us to realize the brevity of life,
so that we may grow in wisdom."
(Psalm 90:12, NLT)

Lord,

We are consumers of time. We are also stewards of time, constantly trying to treat our hours, days and weeks with respect. We try to squeeze as much out of life as we possibly can and then fight to stay balanced.

How we use our time affects all those we work with and our goals. I cannot begin to recall how many times I have found myself paralyzed by not knowing what to do next. I confess to needlessly wasting time by spinning my tires with distractions. I claim Your forgiveness and ask You to teach me how to do it better.

May I realize, deep down, how my lack of planning and forethought causes dismay and frustration in those with whom I work. At the same time I ask You to restrain me from spending so much time in the future that my day-to-day tasks remain undone. May You be my compass, Lord. Set my path before me.

Amen

THE GIFT

OF

ENCOURAGEMENT

EVERYWHERE CHRISTMAS IS CELEBRATED THERE ARE PEOPLE SHOPPING OR making gifts for those they love and care about. This act of gift giving is embedded in the Christmas story itself when wise men brought gold, frankincense and myrrh to lay before Jesus in honour and respect.

As a leader, you may be out looking for gifts to give to those you work with right now, trying to find just the right thing to indicate your appreciation for their loyalty, work effort and contribution to the mission.

Let me share with you the perfect gift leaders can give—encouragement.

The other week, I was asked by one of the Arrow team, "How do you like to be encouraged?" This began my asking the entire team the same question. The answers included: "Small 'gag' gifts that remind you of me," "I like your encouraging messages on my voice mail," "I like it when you notice that I am doing a good job" and "I appreciate it when you praise me in public."

Inspired by this whole experience, I asked Brenda (my wife and best friend) how she liked to be encouraged. "Flowers and diamonds!" she responded, laughing.

Encouragement is such a great gift for leaders to dole out. All it takes is thought and time, yet the impact is lasting. As William Ward said,

117

"Flatter me, and I may not believe you. Criticize me, and I may not like you. Ignore me, and I may not forgive you. Encourage me, and I will not forget you."

Here are some thoughts on how we as leaders can give the gift of encouragement to our coworkers not only at Christmas, but also throughout the year.

- Attune yourself to notice the positive.
- Be very liberal with praise.
- Compliment them frequently, sincerely and publicly.
- Learn the names of their spouses, children and friends; then use them.
- Note their hobbies and special interests and watch for articles that may be of interest to them.
- Work on your own self-image. You cannot love others if you do not like yourself. I find leaders who are not encouraging often need to focus on this.
- Give credit where credit is due.
- Ask, "How can I help?"
- Give appropriate challenges. People get bored when they are not challenged.
- Listen! Really listen to them.

If all it takes is some thought and time for you to encourage others, what is it that prevents you from giving this gift of encouragement more?

A little goes a long way!

"They have been a wonderful encouragement to me, as they have been to you. You must show your appreciation to all who serve so well."
(1 Corinthians 16:18, NLT)

O Lord,

May I be the kind of leader who gives people something to hang on to...a word of encouragement that lingers in their hearts and minds for years. Thank You for the people who have spoken encouragement into my life and helped to shape me into the leader I am today. I pause to bring their names and faces to mind.

Help me to understand those around me well enough to know how they are best encouraged. May I watch them carefully, waiting for every opportunity to encourage them. I want to fill them with courage, Lord, the kind of courage and joy that flows from life in You.

Help me to start close to home. I confess that often those closest to me are the ones who can go for the longest period of time without feeling encouragement from me. Lord, heal the wounds from anything hurtful I have said in the past and bring into light any place where a word of forgiveness is needed before any encouragement can be received. I pause again to let You speak to me.

Amen

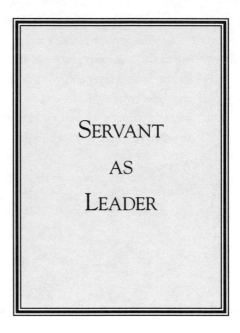

SERVANT

AS

LEADER

A WAVERING ECONOMY OFTEN BRINGS OUT QUESTIONS ABOUT THE VALUE OF investing in leadership development.

Many studies have shown that focused development produces measurable results, so the real question is, "What kind of development is needed?" Is leadership development simply trying to get leaders to be convincing, charismatic, composed and respectful enough to earn the followership of their people?

In the past, organizations used to afford leaders a respect that was automatic. If you had the role, you had the respect. We all know that times have changed. We live in a world where respect is earned, not freely granted.

In these times, most leaders will work hard to gain the respect they need. Some will continue to flourish because of their gifts of charisma and rhetoric, but most will fight the fight. Leadership development has lagged behind the times. Many continue to focus on creating charismatic leaders to invoke the allegiance and servitude of followers. Instead, I would like to propose that when you are developing the leaders around you the focus should be: **Developing the ability and will of the leader to serve rather than be served.**

In 1982, Robert Greenleaf wrote a book that made an indelible mark on my life, entitled, *The Servant as Leader*. This very small book takes only and hour or two to read, yet a lifetime to digest. Robert Greenleaf's compelling insight into the essence of true leadership based on the servant perspective shows how true leaders lead from the front...and the back.

While an emphasis on servant leadership may strike many of us as counter-intuitive when looking at organizational leadership, it makes perfect sense to us in every other relationship context—family, friends and community. The very idea of customer service is a clear example of this. The marketplace intuitively knows that serving customers well leads to desired customer behavior, such as repeat sales and a depth of relationship. Business people involved in leadership development will argue that their staff ought to serve customers well in order to influence their behavior. Yet, the same leaders will focus little attention to serving their colleagues and direct reports.

If your style has been more that of leading from the front, begin to look for ways to really serve those working with you. Try making investments in their development. This may involve formal training, but I am more interested in our pursuit of informal conversations about their life aspirations and dreams.

You can make more friends in two months by becoming interested in other people than you can in two years by trying to get other people interested in you. (Dale Carnegie)

Leadership development should focus on helping leaders identify and pursue their calling and potential. Leaders who also serve encourage the dedication, loyalty and trust that result in strong organizational outcomes.

What can you do today to serve those around you?

"For even the Son of Man came not to be served but to serve others and to give his life as a ransom for many."
(Matthew 20:28, NLT)

O Lord,

I acknowledge that a servant attitude often goes against my grain. I acknowledge that I am prideful, often desiring to be served and admired, rather than serving and admiring those around me. Lord, as I study Your life, I realize that I have it all backwards. Further, I

know that apart from You, I am not capable of serving You and others to the degree I ought. Your way is so much better than my way. Lord, please tap me on the shoulder whenever I slip back into my pride-filled ways.
Humble me, I pray.

Amen

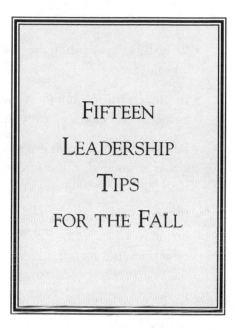

FIFTEEN LEADERSHIP TIPS FOR THE FALL

FOR MANY OF US IN NORTH AMERICA, LATE AUGUST OR EARLY SEPTEMBER IS start up time in our schools, churches and organizations. People are back from holidays and you find yourself "back in business." Here is some leadership advice to help you have a successful year:

- Get yourself a good mentor—someone who can help you navigate around pitfalls. But remember, pitfalls are often a necessary conduit for our growth—something you might use to mentor others one day.

- Hire outside experts. Having a really good accountant, bookkeeper, lawyer or computer person lets you sleep a lot better at night.

- There's always a better, more efficient way to do things. Put time in your life and calendar for creative thinking.

- Focus on creating value for your congregation or customers—those you serve. How can you make their lives better? What will make it really worthwhile for them to give of their time to volunteer or come to that meeting?

- Make sure that you have a loyal group of supporters behind you and spend time with them.

- Be realistic in counting the cost of leadership and take some time for self-care.

- In uncertain economic times, make sure of your revenue assumptions before you start and test them carefully.

- Be creative in reviewing your expense lines on the budget. You would be amazed at how often you can get by without or make do with less.

- Every organization has make-or-break issues. Know what these are in your organization. One example could be: "If certain targets are not met by a certain date, we are finished." Everyone on your team needs to understand and be focused on this pursuit.

- Research, research, research—take some time to do this for your own personal growth and before jumping into anything new.

- Make sure you hire team people with complementary skills and attitudes to your own. Get them to focus on execution of your work or ministry and help them overcome resistance and barriers they face.

- Do not overanalyze situations. Make a decision and get on with the execution.

- Take a risk.

- Persevere. Endure. Keep at it. Do not give up.

- Do not take yourself so seriously. Laugh more. If you can keep a sense of humour it will help give life to your work.

"We also pray that you will be strengthened with all his glorious power so you will have all the endurance and patience you need. May you be filled with joy, always thanking the Father."
(Colossians 1:11-12, NLT)

Lord,

There is great leadership advice to be accessed today. It's everywhere…how to lead and how not to lead. Your word is filled beginning to end with good and bad examples of leadership. Help me to be a multi-dimensional leader, who not only seeks what the world has to offer in leadership advice, but also, what You have to offer me through Your word. Make me a good student of Your word, I pray.

Amen

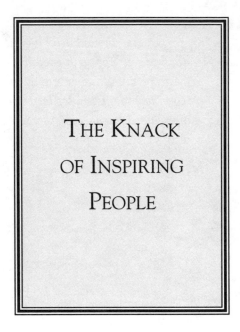

THE KNACK OF INSPIRING PEOPLE

HAVE YOU EVER WONDERED HOW CERTAIN PEOPLE BRING OUT THE BEST IN others? They seem to possess a knack of inspiring people. And this remarkable leadership skill in the art of motivation makes them successful at almost everything they do.

The best leaders are self-confident, good-humoured, treat others with respect and develop contagious enthusiasm in their teams. They smile a lot, seem to feel good about themselves and make others feel good, too. Here are ten things you and I can practice to inspire and motivate:

Be an encourager. Build confidence in your team by complimenting effort, improvement, achievement and success, no matter how small. Taking the time to thank people who help us is a basic courtesy that should apply in all human relations. We all want to be appreciated, and when someone genuinely thanks us, we will follow that person a long way.

Study other people's needs. Real leaders know that if we listen well, people will explain to us what motivates them.

Create an atmosphere where failure is not fatal. It is far more efficient to teach people how to learn from their mistakes, rather than to replace them. A leader knows that the fear of failure can destroy creativity and initiative. I have come to learn that an ability to fail actually makes for long-term success among leaders.

Encourage initiative. People admire and follow a leader who is willing to explore and grow.

Emphasize team. Good leaders do more than build allegiance to themselves. They also build into the team an allegiance to one another. People in these teams will take responsibility for ensuring high standards.

Focus on success. Persuade your team to focus on success, not the obstacles. The leader who believes in success inspires others to follow.

Set high standards. Successful leaders tolerate a considerable amount of individuality, but they insist on high standards and certain core beliefs.

Dream and ask questions. A team leader is one who has a vision, explains it to others, and influences them to follow. Question out loud and give others permission to do the same.

Set an example. Walk the talk. Example matters, not words.

Smile as you communicate. A friendly hello and a smile are successful leadership techniques. There is nothing about you that is more attractive or magnetic than your smile.

Have some fun today and try smiling as an encouragement to those you work with.

> *"When a king's face brightens, it means life;*
> *his favour is like a rain cloud in spring."*
> (Proverbs 16:15, NIV)

Lord Jesus,

When I imagine You with Your disciples, I see laughter and joy, as well as honesty and challenge. You are so compelling. I desire more and more to be like You. I believe that You are the greatest leader to ever walk this earth. Help me to spend more time getting to know You so that I can pass Your inspiring leadership and character along to others.

Amen

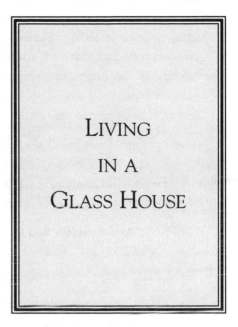

LIVING IN A GLASS HOUSE

IF YOU ARE TO LEAD PEOPLE PROPERLY YOU MUST BE EVER MINDFUL OF THE FACT that you live in a glass house. We need to be diligent about examining our relationships with those around us and our relationship to God. Others will watch our life and work, but we should be more attentive than they are and seek opportunities for improvement. Here are three areas to begin an appraisal:

How is your emotional stability? Have you an even temper that makes proper evaluations of situations? What is your emotional capacity these days? A leader with emotional ups and downs like a camel's back misleads his caravan of followers. Unless those we work with can judge our reactions and forecast our direction, they can potentially fall apart as a team.

Laugh at yourself, your mistakes and foibles. It is a great way to preserve your sanity and keep your balance. But be careful not to laugh with your teammates about your responsibilities or mock the core policies of your organization. What you say and the things you laugh at have special weight because you are the leader.

Keep on learning. This is one of the attractions of being a leader—you can usually make the opportunity to improve personally in knowledge and skills. Challenge yourself to move outside your comfort zone or focus on learning more about a "weak" area of your leadership development. The people who succeed in leadership positions are those who have a thirst for knowledge and go out and secure growth in one way or another, then put it to work.

This appraisal from inside the glass house is from you, for you. I am not asking for you to compare yourself to others. Are you having struggles with jealousy? Feeling like somebody's doing better than you? Well just relax. You are you—not somebody else. Be yourself!

"Listen...and be wise, and keep your heart on the right path."
(Proverbs 23:19, NIV)

Heavenly Father,

I know that as a person in leadership, many eyes are watching me closely. People observe my interactions with team members, with family members, with friends and even my responses to You. I recognize the responsibility and high calling of leadership. And yet, I also know that my first calling is to You. I exist to please You. You are my primary audience, not my followers. You are my audience of One. Help me to strike the balance of loving and blessing You with serving those around me.

Amen

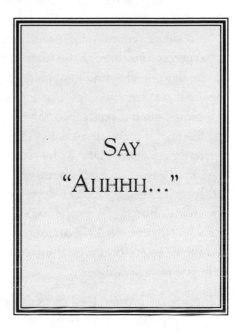

SAY "AIIHHH…"

ON A FAST TRACK TO BURNOUT!

If it has been a long time since you have sat back and just let out a long, satisfied "Ahhhh…" then your goals may also be in jeopardy. When leaders get worn out and enter into frenetic activity, often the people around them get hurt and their organizations begin to flounder. In contrast, I have seen ordinary people do extraordinary things when their spirits are happy and when the team morale is high. So, if you are spinning out of control, then your organization probably is too.

We often do not need a medical opinion to know when we are spinning out of control. Our body usually gives us indicators—we just get very good at ignoring them. The pressures of being a leader today demand so much that we end up sacrificing the very things that bring us great pleasure.

Try asking another leader, "What would you do if you had an extra hour in a day?" Many would like to read a good book and some others would like to take a nap. Better still, ask a leader, "What would you do if you had an extra day in your week?" The most common responses have been: spend time with friends and family, or get outdoors in some activity that promotes better health and perhaps provides a little solitude.

Can I ask, "What brings you great pleasure? When was the last time you were able to do that?"

Pressing circumstances recently caused me to choose to cut back on work to 80 percent for three of the summer months. This decision gave me the gift of one day a week—and I am planning to use it to do some things that bring me great pleasure. Perhaps, I will even explore something new to enjoy.

Now, I am not really into fishing, but a few weeks ago, some friends took me fishing for a couple of days. There was something very appealing about sitting in a boat on a lake with no pager beeping, no computer problems, not having to answer my cell phone or email at all hours. Being outside trolling a fishing line through a lake with good friends made me say "Ahhhh...."

In my mind, I have gone back to that lake several times in the midst of the challenging weeks that followed. It was a very good break. Let me encourage you to find something you can do in the coming months that will help you to say "Ahhhh...."

> *"I know that there is nothing better for [people]*
> *than to be happy and do good while they live."*
> (Ecclesiastes 3:12, NIV)

Lord Jesus,

As I reflect on Your life and leadership, I am reminded afresh of the need for Sabbath moments and times...moments and times of reflection, enjoyment, rest and restoration. Lord, enable me to embrace times of enjoyment and refreshment without guilt. I desire Your wisdom to move forward in my leadership journey with a sense of health and balance...and Your smile of approval.

Thank you, Lord.

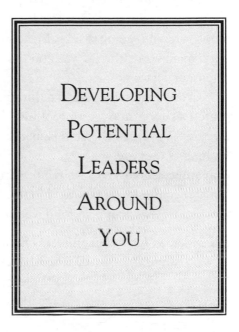

DEVELOPING POTENTIAL LEADERS AROUND YOU

DOES YOUR LEADERSHIP STYLE ALLOW YOU TO DEVELOP NEW LEADERS?

As you think about those working beside you, ask yourself these questions: Are they helping to carry the load for you? Are they growing and developing? Have you seen measurable change? Are you building into their lives?

It has been said, "A good leader inspires other people with confidence in the leader; a great leader inspires them with confidence in themselves." This confidence is instilled by modelling leadership through encouraging them, believing in them, releasing them to achieve their potential, sharing their victories, and trusting them.

The organization, church, denomination or business you serve would be transformed if you were to identify 20 percent of its most promising potential leaders and spend 80 percent of your leadership development resources and nurturing time with them.

You must be willing to pour your life into others and commit to growing leadership within your organization. My guess is that you already feel stretched in too many different directions. Me too. Yet we, as leaders, set the tone for leadership development within the entire organization. Effective leaders develop potential leaders.

Developing leaders also requires a great deal of security as well as sacrifice. It will cost potential leaders time and effort, so make sure they know what it is going to take. Make sure they understand that you are asking for a commitment to growth and that it is going to stretch them far beyond their comfort zone.

One of the most difficult things in developing promising leaders is to watch a person stop growing. When the potential leader you are developing decides to go no further, remember that you are only called to help them for as long as they are willing to keep growing. When they choose to stop, you can still celebrate their growth to that point and remain friends—but move on and continue developing others.

So, what is your plan for developing potential leaders around you?

"In fact, in his public ministry he never taught without using parables;
but afterward, when he was alone with his disciples,
he explained everything to them."
(Mark 4:34, NLT)

Lord God,

Thank You for sending Your Son, Jesus, to be our model for investing deeply in others. When Jesus walked this earth, He was constantly investing in people around Him…some more deeply than others. Lord, please show me the people You would have me invest in. Help me to be as intentional about developing others as You were and are. Lord, once You have shown me who I need to invest in, please grant me Your wisdom and skill in the mentoring process as I pray through all aspects of that relationship. I realize that I cannot do this well without You guiding me every step of the way.

Amen

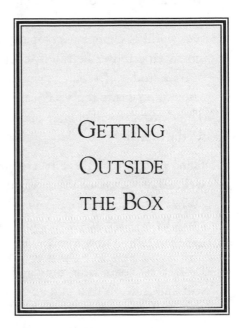

GETTING
OUTSIDE
THE BOX

WHAT DOES IT TAKE TODAY TO GET YOU "THINKING OUTSIDE THE BOX?" Often, it is a crisis of some sort, but all leaders should utilize creative thinking on an ongoing basis. Chances are that one of the reasons you are in leadership is because of an ability to think creatively and act on it. But what about today?

Can radical thinking and brainstorming be done in your work environment? The typical organization today is a fast-paced environment with a structured corporate culture. These cultures usually require quick, sometimes shortsighted answers, which are heavily influenced by resource constraints and political-hierarchical power. How is effective and creative thinking encouraged (or even accepted) in that kind of environment? The answer is that it's not!

Creative thinking often creates stress among some coworkers, but do not let this dissuade you from thinking outside the box. Often, a "fire fighting" approach to solving an endless string of problems engages all our time, leaving little for creative thinking.

Here are three ideas to force you to see beyond the box:

Make a list of all of the assumptions you currently function with as an organization and then challenge every single one of them. Our world is changing so rapidly that assumptions made five years ago may no longer be valid—even though they govern the way you operate today. In our organization, we recently challenged an assumption made ten years earlier and found it was invalid today. This discovery will change our future direction and will potentially do the same for you.

Hand pick two or three trusted leaders who know your situation well. Share some of your personal leadership challenges and ask, "What would you do if you were leading in my place?" Listen carefully to their responses and look for synergies. Maybe you will hear something new that you have never considered before.

Project 50 years from now and envision what your organization will look like. Will it still exist? What will it be doing? How many staff will there be? What kind of impact will it have on the community, country or world? Now review your current schedule and ask if it reflects this future reality? Is there a change you should make to your life and work schedule this year to enable you to do the thinking and strategizing necessary to move your organization or ministry in this direction?

Many of us get caught up in managing for yesterday's conditions, because yesterday is where we got our experiences and had our successes. But leadership is about tomorrow, not yesterday. So go on—get outside the box. Doctor's orders!

> *"Do not conform any longer to the pattern of this world,*
> *but be transformed by the renewing of your mind.*
> *Then you will be able to test and approve what God's will is—*
> *his good, pleasing and perfect will."*
> (Romans 12:2, NIV)

Father God,

You are the great Creator. I see Your touch everywhere I look. You have also created me in Your image…as a creative being. I ask You to help me, as a leader, to reflect Your creativity in my thinking and my actions. Through the prodding of Your Spirit, allow me to see and understand what prevents or stifles Your creativity in my life and work. May I be released from that which blocks Your desires for me as a leader. May I be freed up to reflect Your creativity over and over.

Amen

COPING WITH EXPECTATIONS

HAVE YOU EVER HAD A PHYSICAL INJURY WHERE YOU WERE IN PAIN BUT HAD trouble pinpointing the source? Most leaders have the same difficulty with expectations.

How does a leader assess internal expectations and set realistic goals? Here are a few ideas I have found helpful. It helps me to identify the various roles in my life and then complete sentences like:

> "In my relationship with my wife, I expect to…"
> "As a father, I expect to…"
> "As a team leader, I will not be satisfied with my leadership unless I…"
> "The most important goal I have for myself personally is…"

List all of the expectations you are feeling right now and ask yourself: Where does that expectation come from? When, where and why did I accept that expectation for myself? Does my board or supervisor "really" expect that of me, or is this mostly coming from within? In consultation with many leaders, I find that most of us expect much more of ourselves than our constituencies do.

138

Do you have some unconscious motivators acting in your life? The most common are fear, anger and guilt. Seek out a friend that you trust and can disclose to. Often, it helps so much to just voice these feelings aloud.

Allow yourself to examine how closely your sense of self-worth is wrapped up in fulfilling your expectations. Most leaders discover—through pain, unfortunately—that self-worth comes from God alone. Leaders can almost kill themselves with discipline, trying to achieve their own goals and expectations—and then, after achieving them, feel completely empty inside. Often, they set some new achievement to pursue—all in the search of misplaced self-worth. Test yourself: try going for two weeks without making a single reference to one of your achievements or accomplishments.

When our work and our worth come from God, His grace covers us when we fail. It is a great position to lead from.

"But the Lord said to her, 'My dear Martha, you are worried and upset over all these details! There is only one thing worth being concerned about. Mary has discovered it, and it will not be taken away from her.'"
(Luke 10:41,42, NLT)

Lord,

How do I go about striking a balance between setting good, godly, and worthy expectations and letting go of unrealistic expectations, which are not from You at all? Please help me to rightly discern my self-expectations and motives. Help me to be honest with myself before You and others.

Amen

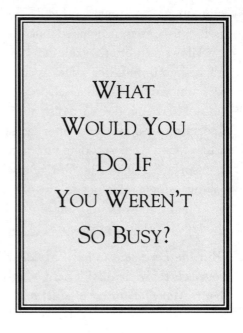

WHAT WOULD YOU DO IF YOU WEREN'T SO BUSY?

RECENTLY, I WAS SITTING IN A WISE FRIEND'S SUNROOM WHEN HE ASKED, "Carson, what would you be doing if you were not having to spend so much of your time raising support for developing leaders?"

His question opened my mind to ideas that had not surfaced for a long time. I found myself rattling off about six initiatives I would just love to be pursuing—ideas that filled me with energy and hope. It felt like the top of my head was opened up and I was freed for that moment to dream again. I thought instantly of aspects of leadership that were not getting attention— projects that could accelerate us moving toward accomplishing our vision.

In your business, what is not getting done? As a parent, are there things you would like to do with your children that you have been too busy to attend to? As a friend, are you too busy to pursue friendship at a depth you desire? How much time do you spend working in your ministry, rather than on your ministry?

I spoke with an Arrow leader this week who described his 16-hour days. Together, we were able to identify over 60 percent of his time being spent on activities that have built up over time and were now hindering his ability to actually lead the organization through their current challenges. Many leaders lose their sense of joy by being consumed with activities that take away from their ability to lead. The fun is gone.

If your leadership time is spent on busy work that could be delegated then it is time to pause and reevaluate. Here are three steps that can help:

Plan a 24-hour retreat. Spend time in solitude and outline the projects you would like to work on, but currently have no time to address. Pray, asking the Lord to instill a renewed view of stewardship of your time. Plan at least half a day each month for this exercise, or the pattern of busyness will repeat itself quickly.

Fill out a two-week calendar of your schedule and allow a trusted friend, your spouse or perhaps member of your team to objectively review your use of leadership time.

Identify one thing you can stop doing all together, and three things you can delegate to someone else who can do it 85 percent as well as you could. This will help you to let go of some things in which you might be currently enmeshed.

Every time you leave the steering wheel of your organization to do tasks that God has prepared others to do, you leave the organization without anyone driving. So it is important to ask, "What would you like to be doing if you weren't so busy?"

"What you are doing is not good. You and these people who come to you will only wear yourselves out. The work is too heavy for you; you cannot handle it alone...You must be the people's representative before God and bring their disputes to him. Teach them...and show them the way to live and the duties they are to perform. But select capable [people]...who fear God, trustworthy [people]... and appoint them as officials over thousands, hundreds, fifties and tens. Have them serve...the people at all times, but have them bring every difficult case to you; the simple cases they can decide themselves. That will make your load lighter, because they will share it with you."
(Exodus 18:17-22, NIV)

Leaders can never dodge the difficult cases, so go find those who can be appointed to handle simpler duties.

Father God,

Thank you for Your word...for its wisdom, practicality, inspiration, challenge, encouragement and nourishment. In my leadership calling, I acknowledge that Your word sustains me and propels me forward. I sometimes get moving so fast, that I forget to give Your word the attention that it deserves and things start to unravel for me, sometimes to the point of crisis. Help me deal with busyness and distractions by trusting those around me enough to delegate...help me to lead well. After all, that is what you have called me to.

Amen

Risk Tomorrow's Challenge

Leaders provide a stimulus for change wherever we serve. We call attention to the possibilities; we take risks and encourage others to initiate change. Leaders encourage their staff to experiment with various methods to meet needs in their community. Or do we?

Have you stopped taking risks?

Perhaps "but" statements like these have caused you to stop taking risks:

"But I am afraid." We face fear every day, and when faced with the possibility of taking a risk, all of our fears surface. It is important to examine every single one of these fears and learn from them before making a significant "risk" decision. *But,* once you have examined all the facts and made your decision, then stop fearing and move ahead, knowing that God is completely capable of doing a course correction if necessary.

"But I have been through so much in my past." At Mount Rushmore, South Dakota, are the carved figures of four great U.S. presidents. The artist, Gutzon Borglum, when asked how he did it, modestly replied, "Well, those figures were there for forty million years. All I had to do was dynamite 400,000 tons of granite to bring them into view." This is a vivid picture of what God does with Christian leaders. He is constantly removing the debris, the impediments, so that the real you can emerge. He works in us to help us fulfill our destiny and calling, to be productive and accomplish the task He has ordained for us.

"But I am not sure what others would think." If you are surrounded by those who belittle your ambitions, you will seldom rise above their expectations of you. But if you surround yourself with some great people, you will begin to feel and act great.

"But I am really comfortable right now." It is so easy for leaders to drift towards comfort and security—almost preferring security to making ourselves available to what God would fully like to do with our lives. Quit hanging onto today's comfort. If you stay hooked to security today, it will prevent you from realizing what God would do in your life tomorrow.

Robert Frost wrote, "Two roads diverged in a wood, and...I took the one less travelled by, and that has made all the difference." What road are you on?

> *"By faith Abraham...obeyed and went, even though he did not know where he was going."*
> (Hebrews 11:8, NIV)

Gracious Father,

Give me courage to face my fears. Help me to risk for You...even if it means being a "fool" for the name of Christ.

Amen

HIRING A LEADER

THE MOST CRITICAL CHALLENGE FACING CHRISTIAN ORGANIZATIONS IS A shortage of good leaders.

Simply put, leaders can make or break a ministry. Unfortunately, great leaders are in short supply in our day. The calibre of your organization's leadership team can mean the difference between scraping and scratching just to get by and redefining the vision to do huge things for God.

Recognizing and admitting that your ministry has a shortage of good leaders is easy. Understanding the nature of that shortage and finding new leadership is difficult. I am frequently asked how do we identify a leader. Great question! To answer that question, allow me to pose another. Are there certain developmental experiences that are common among leaders we could actually look for? Yes, I think so!

Most leaders I speak with have had some experiences in their formative years that were crucial in their development as a leader. They include:

Personal crisis. Leaders often have had some kind of a crisis, emotional or physical in nature, which forced them to take responsibility for themselves and sometimes for others as well. Dealing with crises improves an individual's capacity to cope with future unusual situations. Often, a background like this can be misinterpreted as a weakness, but most leaders have had their metal forged in the furnace of crisis.

Early role models. When asked about significant people in their lives, leaders invariably mention parents, mentors or another significant figure that provided major encouragement and inspiration for them to be people of faith and integrity.

Early success. Leaders begin leading as children. A good track record, experienced from a young age, provided continual opportunities, which gave these leaders the encouragement to risk again and again.

In trying to find a potential leader, be sure to pray for wisdom. Then, listen carefully as you ask intentional questions related to these three developmental experiences.

"Jesse had seven of his sons pass before Samuel, but Samuel said to him, 'The LORD has not chosen these.' So he asked Jesse, 'Are these all the sons you have?' 'There is still the youngest,' Jesse answered, 'but he is tending the sheep.' Samuel said, 'Send for him...Rise and anoint him; he is the one.'"
(1 Samuel 16:10-12, NIV)

Lord God,

The old adage "Don't judge a book by its cover" seems to apply in the area of hiring leaders. May I not be guilty of passing by Your choice because I too harshly judge a person. Leadership is so important to You and to our world to miss out on the right leaders at the right time. Go before me. Give me Your eyes to see and Your ears to hear Your will for this team.

Amen

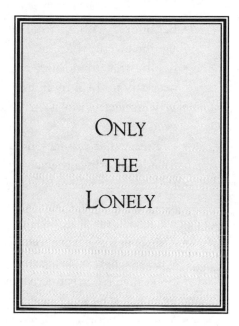

ONLY THE LONELY

"IT'S LONELY AT THE TOP." THIS OFTEN-QUOTED LEADERSHIP MOTTO IS TRUE TO some extent because, while a good leader can delegate tasks to others, the burden of responsibility ultimately falls on his or her shoulders.

Most leaders confess a deep sense of loneliness, although most of us work hard at wallpapering over the cracks caused by it. We overwork to convince the world of our worth. We flit from one superficial engagement to another to give the impression that we have lots of friends. For some leaders, the pain of loneliness becomes so familiar that it resembles numbness.

As I wondered about the health of a lonely lifestyle, I did some research and found some surprising results. Did you know that lonely people have impaired immune systems, making them more vulnerable to colds and other illnesses? Lonely leaders also turn to the Internet in increasing numbers, leading to problems with depression, escapism and addictions. Alcohol, drug abuse and/or pornography intensify feelings of loneliness. Having many "functional" relationships at work can also distract us from pursuing healthy, intimate relationships.

WHAT CAN YOU DO?

- Be honest with yourself and survey the relationships of significance in your life.
- Realize that friendships and social bonds with others are a necessity for healthy living.
- Writing letters is a start. Talking to people on the phone is even better.
- Consider that you may have a "learning deficit" in forming friendships with others.
- Perhaps start a Lonely Hearts' Club for Christian leaders—getting together occasionally with others who understand the loneliness of leadership.
- Think about getting some therapy as a way to acquire the skills you may be lacking.
- Seek medical treatment for severe anxiety or depression brought on by loneliness.
- Make the effort to join a small group for leisure, support and fun.
- Limit use of the Internet as an anonymous source of interaction.

Loneliness attacks the senses. Leaders feel isolated, rejected and abandoned, like no one really understands. However, loneliness can build something into our character that few other experiences allow. Mostly, loneliness teaches us that we all need love—to give and receive love.

> *"A person standing alone can be attacked and defeated,*
> *but two can stand back-to-back and conquer.*
> *Three are even better, for a triple-braided cord*
> *is not easily broken."*
> (Ecclesiastes 4:12, NLT)

O Lord,

I acknowledge that there are times when I feel the weight and responsibility of leadership, and in those times I feel lonely. I believe that, at times, Jesus felt the burden of loneliness, too. God, may my first response to loneliness be to turn to You. And then I ask You for courage to take the necessary steps to once again enjoy fullness and freedom of relationship in You.

Amen

CHANGE
NEVER
LETS UP

CHANGE NEVER LETS UP. IT KEEPS COMING—IN YOUR PERSONAL LIFE, BUSINESS, family or organization. But you can use change to take advantage of opportunities, so it's critical to enhance your resilience while facing daily change.

To do so, you need to develop six characteristics: be prayerful, positive, focused, flexible, organized and proactive.

Prayerful leaders recognize that what we experience as "change" has already passed through the Father's hands. We must turn to God for wisdom and guidance. Leaders must be able to view patterns in the organization as if they were on a balcony. Prayer is the first requirement for "getting on the balcony." Prayer distances our ego and personal perspective from what is happening on the field of action.

Positive leaders develop the ability to view life as challenging, dynamic and filled with opportunities. They appreciate the dangers and threats in change, but are not overwhelmed by them. They also seek information about the change.

Focused leaders determine where they are headed and stick to the goal so that barriers encountered along the way do not become insurmountable.

Blocks, or obstacles, require attention if they affect the goal. Otherwise, do not put energy into them.

Flexible leaders are open to different options when faced with uncertainty. They recognize their personal strengths and weaknesses and know when to accept internal or external limitations and when to push past them.

Organized leaders develop structured approaches to manage ambiguity. They set priorities, but can renegotiate them if needed. Organized leaders also know when to ask others for help.

Proactive leaders work with change rather than defend against it. They learn from change and can creatively reframe a situation that is changing. They do not just sit there!

"The faithful love of the LORD never ends! His mercies never cease. Great is his faithfulness; his mercies begin afresh each morning."
(Lamentations 3:22-23, NLT)

Lord God,

In a world that is constantly changing, I remember that You are the same...yesterday, today and forever. You are the constant when all else is changing. May I embrace this constantly changing world You have created with prayer, a positive attitude, focus, flexibility, organization and a proactive mindset. Thank you for the life-giving aspect of change...I shudder to think of the alternative. Truly, Your mercies are NEW every morning.

Amen

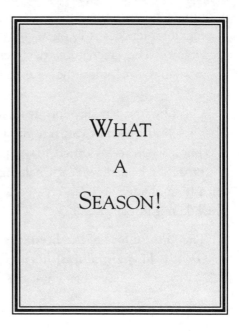

WHAT

A

SEASON!

IS YOUR WORLD LIKE THAT OF THE RED QUEEN FROM *ALICE IN WONDERLAND*? She describes it like this: "Now here, you see, it takes all the running you can do to keep in the same place. If you want to get somewhere else, you must run at least twice as fast as that."

The stresses of leadership in some seasons can hurry us along in life to the point where it seems we cannot move to a new place. All the while, most Christian leaders will not discard a second-rate version of what Jesus really intended for us. Yet, it is important for us as leaders to see that our needs are cared for.

Jesus can relate to all seasons. He was often very busy, but was never hurried. His schedule was full of ministry activity followed by His withdrawing for prayer and solitude. Jesus was never so busy that His life-giving connection with the Father was detached. Has that been true of you this past year?

Like me, you may be taking time right now to plan and forecast vision. As you do, let me suggest you use a calendar where you can see the year at a glance. Write in family dates first—special days, times and vacations. Then, add the "givens" for you in your work, such as classes, board meetings, annual events and special projects. You will suddenly be able to see your demanding seasons. Next, look at the days in between and plan to observe a regular rhythm of withdrawing from the busyness to care for yourself. Mark those days into the calendar right now—it may be the only chance of ensuring you will care for yourself in the coming year. These can be good times to focus on spiritual disciplines such as prayer, fasting and solitude.

We can try all sorts of methods to take care of ourselves, but God insists that we look to Him alone for the meeting of our needs. So, give God some time in your calendar—because He wants to meet your every need.

> **"And my God will supply all your needs according to
> His riches in glory in Christ Jesus."**
> (Philippians 4:19, NAS)

Heavenly Father,

When life gets too busy and chaotic, enable me to be intentional about pulling back and embracing the spiritual disciplines of prayer and solitude and even fasting. This seems counterintuitive when I am stressed and feeling burned out and yet this was Jesus' pattern. Enable me to pattern my own leadership after the greatest leader to ever walk the face of this earth.

Amen

KEY THEMES INDEX

CASTLE QUAY BOOKS

OTHER CASTLE QUAY TITLES INCLUDE:

Bent Hope (Tim Huff)
The Beautiful Disappointment (Colin McCartney)
The Cardboard Shack Beneath the Bridge (Tim Huff)
Certainty (Grant Richison)
The Chicago Healer (Paul Boge)
Dancing with Dynamite (Tim Huff)
Deciding to Know God in a Deeper Way (Sam Tita)
The Defilers (Deborah Gyapong)
Father to the Fatherless (Paul Boge)
I Sat Where They Sat (Arnold Bowler)
Jesus and Caesar (Brian Stiller)
Keep On Standing (Darlene Polachic)
The Leadership Edge (Elaine Stewart-Rhude)
Making Your Dreams Your Destiny (Judy Rushfeldt)
Mere Christianity (Michael Coren)
One Smooth Stone (Marcia Lee Laycock)
Red Letter Revolution (Colin McCartney)
Seven Angels for Seven Days (Angelina Fast-Vlaar)
Stop Preaching and Start Communicating (Tony Gentilucci)
Through Fire & Sea (Marilyn Meyers)
To My Family (Diane Roblin-Lee)
Vision that Works (David Collins)
Walking Towards Hope (Paul Boge)
The Way They Should Go (Kirsten Femson)
You Never Know What You Have Till You Give It Away (Brian Stiller)

BAYRIDGE BOOKS TITLES:

Counterfeit Code: Answering The Da Vinci Code Heresies (Jim Beverley)
More Faithful Than We Think (Lloyd Mackey)
Save My Children (Emily Wierenga)
Wars Are Never Enough: The Joao Matwawana Story (John F. Keith)

For more information and to explore the rest of our titles visit
www.castlequaybooks.com

About Arrow Leadership...

Are you leading, yet sensing the need to sharpen your skills? To build your leadership toolbox? Is leadership your calling? Would you like a mentor to help assess your needs and then walk you through an individualized development plan? Maybe we should talk...

Good leadership decisions often start with access to the right network. Today a global network of Christian leaders have gone through a transformational leadership development process known as the Arrow Leadership Program. Imagine having access to a lifetime of resource and wisdom from world class experts and peers.

The world is a very different place today. There is no "one size fits all" solution. That is why Arrow's highly individualized, multi-layered process is so effective. Our mentoring program is recognized academically by top colleges but perhaps more importantly Arrow is known for being intentional, spiritual and relevant. The most common words used by alumni of their Arrow experience—pivotal, transformational, and networked.

Do you long to be the leader God desires you to be? A leader with a finger on the pulse of your ministry or business? A leader that can operate in a high performance environment and that can inspire a team to go beyond expectations?

Begin now and enquire at www.arrowleadership.org or call us in North America toll free 1.877.262.7769.

You will walk away from this experience a different person, a different leader.